ZOOS

of the MIDWEST

AN ANIMAL PHOTO BOOK
AND TRAVEL GUIDE TO
28 MIDWESTERN ZOOS

STEPHEN TOOTHMAN

★ DEDICATION ★

First and foremost, this book is dedicated to the wonderful zoos it has been my privilege to visit over the last couple of years as I have worked on this project. This book grew out of a personal quest to visit all the zoos within easy driving range of my house in Des Moines, Iowa. It had been my longtime plan to make a tour of all the zoos in my surrounding states. That plan never quite got off the ground. But in the spring and summer of 2018, I drove to all the zoos on my Midwest zoos list except for the two in Chicago. And in 2019, I visited those two remaining zoos. I would like to thank all the people who have accompanied me on my quest, whether in person or by just following my adventures online. Without you, it would not have been nearly so much fun.

Snow leopard from Minnesota Zoo in Apple Valley, MN

Written by Stephen Toothman • All photographs by Stephen Toothman
Cover and book design by Domini Dragoone • Edited by Alison Duncan

Front cover image: Amur Tiger — Sedgwick County Zoo (Wichita, KS)
Back cover image: Asian Small-Clawed Otter — Minnesota Zoo (Apple Valley, MN)

ISBN-10: 1-7343678-0-6 • ISBN-13: 978-1-7343678-0-5

★ ACKNOWLEDGMENTS ★

I WOULD LIKE TO ACKNOWLEDGE THE HOSPITALITY AND ASSISTANCE OF THE 28 ZOOS COVERED IN THIS BOOK, STARTING WITH MY HOME ZOO, BLANK PARK ZOO, IN DES MOINES, IOWA.

THE OTHER ZOOS INCLUDED IN THIS BOOK ARE:

Bramble Park Zoo — Watertown, South Dakota

Chahinkapa Zoo — Wahpeton, North Dakota

Como Park Zoo and Conservatory — Saint Paul, Minnesota

Dakota Zoo — Bismarck, North Dakota

David Traylor Zoo of Emporia — Emporia, Kansas

Dickerson Park Zoo — Springfield, Missouri

Great Bend-Brit Spaugh Zoo — Great Bend, Kansas

Great Plains Zoo — Sioux Falls, South Dakota

Hemker Park and Zoo — Freeport, Minnesota

Henry Doorly Zoo and Aquarium — Omaha, Nebraska

Hutchinson Zoo — Hutchinson, Kansas

Kansas City Zoo — Kansas City, Missouri

Lake Superior Zoo — Duluth, Minnesota

Lee G. Simmons Conservation Park and Wildlife Safari — Ashland, Nebraska

Lee Richardson Zoo — Garden City, Kansas

Lincoln Children's Zoo — Lincoln, Nebraska

Minnesota Zoo — Apple Valley, Minnesota

Red River Zoo — Fargo, North Dakota

Riverside Discovery Center — Scottsbluff, Nebraska

Rolling Hills Zoo — Salina, Kansas

Roosevelt Park Zoo — Minot, North Dakota

Saint Louis Zoo — Saint Louis, Missouri

Sedgwick County Zoo — Wichita, Kansas

Sunset Zoo — Manhattan, Kansas

Tanganyika Wildlife Park — Goddard, Kansas

Topeka Zoo and Conservation Center — Topeka, Kansas

Wright Park Zoo — Dodge City, Kansas

★ INTRODUCTION: MY QUEST ★

I love zoos. It is no secret to my family and friends that an outing to the zoo is one of my favorite ways to spend a day. Funnily enough, my quest to visit all the zoos of the Midwest started many years ago when I was discussing ideas for a fun, romantic trip with a potential partner. The partner did not last, but the idea of visiting all these zoos on a week-long tour stayed with me over the years. It was a simple plan: start with Minnesota Zoo and then go counter-clockwise around the Midwest. The next stop would be Sioux Falls, followed by Omaha, then Kansas City, Saint Louis, and finally Chicago, ending there with a two-day zoo extravaganza. As a cap to the entire tour, the last zoo on the journey would be my home zoo here in Des Moines, Iowa, Blank Park Zoo.

As time passed, I never had an opportunity to put the plan into action, but I never stopped dreaming about it. Then in 2017, a birthday purchase of a new Canon camera, an EOS Rebel T6, spurred a renewed interest in photography—and would be the impetus for a new plan. In the spring of 2018, finding myself childless for a weekend and having no other plans, I drove down to Kansas City for the day. I brought my camera and went to the Kansas City Zoo. I had such a good time on this day trip that it spawned another day trip and then another. By the end of that summer, I had been to all the zoos on my list, except the two zoos in Chicago.

That summer of 2018 is when the second driver of this quest presented itself. It was the middle of July, and I had just returned from another day trip. My friend and cooking buddy, Arif, asked me what I planned to do with all the pictures I had taken. I laughed and joked that maybe I would write a book about my adventures, Zoos of the Midwest. This

planted an idea that did not leave my brain either. I started doing research on books about zoos and how I could organize my trips into a coherent whole.

The first step was coming up with a definitive list of zoos. I settled on the list from the Association of Zoos and Aquariums (AZA). As an independent accrediting organization for zoos and aquariums, the AZA ensures that facilities meet the highest standards for animal care and welfare, among its many other activities. Of the 245 organizations accredited by the organization at the time, 159 were zoos across the United States. To this list I added the zoos accredited by the other major zoo organization, the Zoological Association of America (ZAA). That added 23 more zoos to my list. I also included two more zoos on my list that were not accredited. The first was Niabi Zoo in Coal Valley, Illinois. They had been accredited by the AZA in the past and were working hard to regain their accreditation. It was one of the zoos I had visited in 2018, and I had been impressed by their efforts. I also added Great Bend Zoo in Great Bend, Kansas, which, like Niabi Zoo, had been accredited by the AZA in the past.

Now that I had my list of zoos covering the whole country, I started to analyze how to break it down into books and how it would then break down into trips to visit all these zoos. I knew since I had already started visiting zoos in the Midwest, that would be my first book. I narrowed it down further to seven Midwestern states: Iowa, Minnesota, Missouri, Kansas, Nebraska, South Dakota, and North Dakota. This was the smallest of the six regions I had split my big list into with only 28 zoos in total. It took two summers, but I managed to take pictures at all of them. All that was left to do was to organize

African crowned crane from Lincoln Children's Zoo in Lincoln, NE

everything and write this book—no small feat. Eventually I will make trips to all six of the regions on the list to take pictures, and I plan to write a book about each region as well. Next up I will tackle what I call the Great Lakes region and after that I will work on the South.

This book is organized into two sections. The first section, which I call the "Guide," includes some information about each of the zoos I visited. I look at the history of each of the zoos, their current conservation efforts, and key visiting information, including how to become a member of the zoo, visiting hours, contact information, and pictures of some of the animals they care for and protect in the zoo. The second section, the "Photo Book," is a collection of pictures of some of the animals the zoos have in common, such as tigers and lions and bears, oh my! It tells a bit more about the animals, their conservation status, and a bit about my experiences with taking pictures of them at these zoos.

Now, on with the show!

★ WHY ZOOS ARE ★ IMPORTANT TODAY

I often hear from people I talk to about my project that they do not understand why anyone would want to visit a zoo. They usually add that they think of zoos as being places with animals in cages. Jim Breheny, Director of the Bronx Zoo, put it this way in the introduction to Animal Planet's show *The Zoo,* "ask someone to draw a picture of a zoo, and they will most likely draw an animal in a cage, and we must change that view. In the modern zoo, an animal in a cage is rarely the case anymore. Most modern enclosures are built to mimic the natural environment where the animal lives and provide both public and private spaces for the animals."

While the mission of having animals on exhibit is important because it connects the general public to the wild and educates them on the importance of conservation, it is not the most essential mission zoos have. The most crucial mission is conservation itself, both of the animals in their care and their brethren in the wild. The AZA has raised over $200 million a year to support conservation efforts around the planet. And by buying this book, you are helping to contribute to those efforts, too. A portion of the proceeds from each book sale will go to the zoos featured in this book and support the conservation efforts of the AZA and the ZAA.

In many ways, zoos have become the front line in the battle to save endangered species and protect the natural environment they rely on to live. Conservation efforts do not benefit an endangered species alone, but that animal's whole ecosystem as well. That means that even though the Amur tiger is the focus of worldwide conservation efforts, an entire range of plants and animals benefit from the effort, like the Asian black bear and sika deer who share its habitat.

Zoos are at the forefront of reintroduction efforts, like the one for the black-footed ferret, which had gone extinct in the wild. This species was brought back from the brink by a coalition of organizations, including some of the zoos featured in this book. The ferret went from no wild populations in 1987 to having a population of over 1200 in the wild in 2013 spread over more than 20 different sites across the United States, Canada, and Mexico. This is just one of the many success stories in which zoos have played a part in helping preserve and protect animals in the wild.

Zoos are not just focused on faraway places; they work locally as well. My home zoo, Blank Park Zoo, sponsors several local conservation efforts, like the Plant.Grow.Fly. program. The program is designed to help teach about the value of pollinators and things people can do to help preserve and protect them. One of the program's significant initiatives is encouraging people to plant pollinator-friendly gardens. The zoo provides lots of information on what to plant and how to plant them, and it provides a place for people to register their garden online. Efforts like these are essential because they bring conservation home to the communities they serve.

Opposite: Sumatran orangutan from Como Park Zoo in Saint Paul, MN (top), fossa from Lincoln Children's Zoo in Lincoln, NE (bottom left), scimitar-horned oryx from Kansas City Zoo in Kansas City, MO (bottom right)

ZOOS

Table of Contents

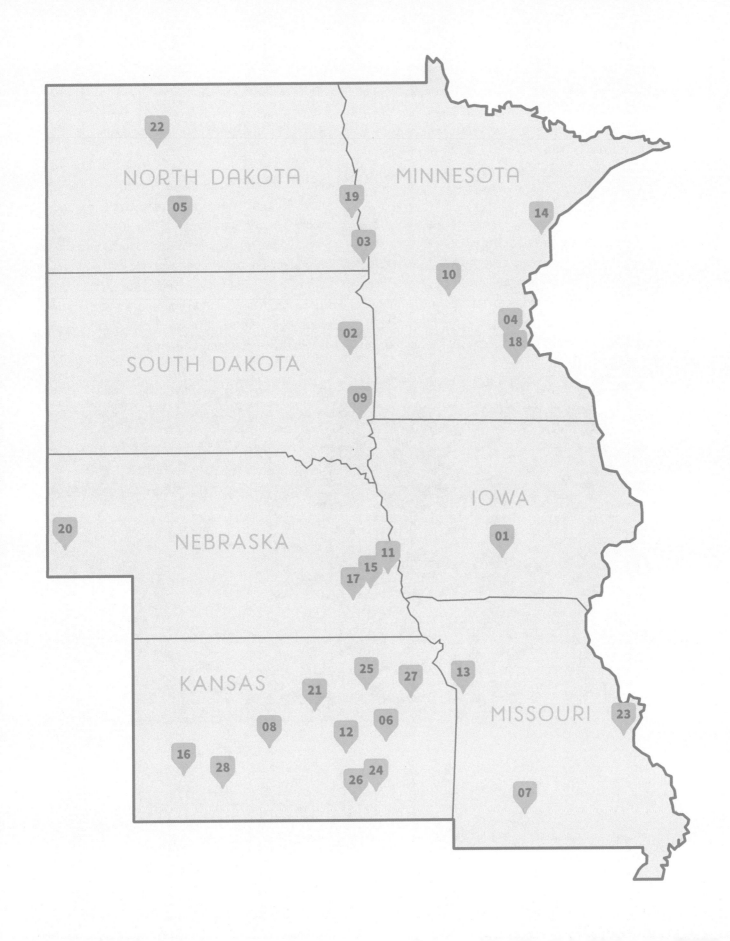

MIDWESTERN UNITED STATES

★ BLANK PARK ZOO ★

Des Moines, Iowa

Blank Park Zoo began life as the Des Moines Children's Zoo in 1966. It had a miniature train, Monkey Island, barnyard, and a petting zoo. It gradually declined over the years until, in 1986, it reopened as Blank Park Zoo. It has been a significant tourist attraction in Des Moines ever since, with over 480,000 people visiting the zoo in 2015.

The zoo currently features animals from around the world, including endangered eastern black rhinos. It has an all-season aviary connected to the entrance complex, meaning it can even be enjoyed during trips to the zoo in the winter. There is an impressive African exhibit with elands, giraffes, and many other species. All combined, the zoo manages 104 separate species and over 1400 individual animals on a 22-acre site. It is accredited by the Association of Zoos and Aquariums (AZA) and has been reaccredited at each renewal.

The zoo is involved in several Species Survival Plans, including those for the ring-tailed lemur, snow leopard, Amur tiger, Japanese macaque, golden-headed lion tamarin, Panamanian golden frog, and red panda. In addition to this, the zoo has several other conservation and research programs. One of its significant outreach efforts is the Wild Bunch program, which is composed of staff and volunteers who work on local conservation projects in the surrounding community.

Harbor seal from Blank Park Zoo in Des Moines, IA

PLAN YOUR VISIT

ADDRESS: 7401 SW 9th Street, Des Moines, IA 50315
MAIN PHONE: (515) 285-4722
WEBSITE: www.blankparkzoo.com
MEMBERSHIP: www.blankparkzoo.com/membership

HOURS

OCTOBER–APRIL: Sun–Sat: 10:00 am–4:00 pm
MAY–SEPTEMBER: Sun–Sat: 9:00 am–5:00 pm
CLOSED: Thanksgiving, Christmas Eve, Christmas Day, and New Year's Day

Kori bustard (above) and lowland nyala (below) from Blank Park Zoo in Des Moines, IA

★ BRAMBLE PARK ZOO ★

Watertown, South Dakota

💬 **Bramble Park Zoo was founded in 1912 when** Frank Bramble donated a collection of pheasants and waterfowl to the city of Watertown. The zoo moved to its current location in 1940, and additional exhibits were constructed by the Works Progress Administration (WPA). The Lake Area Zoological Society was founded in 1972 as a membership organization for the zoo. With its support, the zoo continued to expand and was accredited in 1993. Since then the zoo has continued to grow and improve their exhibits.

🐻 **From its humble origins, the zoo has grown** to now include animals from all over the world. The Terry Redlin Environmental Center at the main entrance is home to an impressive collection of aquariums and small animal exhibits. Other areas of the zoo include Jaguar Junction and a very nice children's zoo. On its 15-acre site, the zoo manages 680 animals from 120 different species. It is accredited by the AZA and has been reaccredited at each renewal. In 2018, it received a Quarter Century Award from the AZA celebrating its 25th year of continuous approval.

🍃 **Bramble Park Zoo participates in numerous** Species Survival Plans, including those for the De Brazza's monkey, three-toed sloth, and swift fox. In local conservation efforts, the zoo has run a raptor rehabilitation center for over 25 years that treats and releases hundreds of birds of prey, including bald eagles. It also runs a successful program fostering wood ducks, which are common to the Prairie Pothole Region where the zoo is located.

Lionfish from Bramble Zoo in Watertown, SD

PLAN YOUR VISIT

ADDRESS: 800 10th Street NW, Watertown, SD 57201
MAIN PHONE: (605) 882-6269
WEBSITE: www.brambleparkzoo.com
MEMBERSHIP: www.brambleparkzoo.com/membership

HOURS

LABOR DAY–MEMORIAL DAY: Sun–Sat: 10:00 am–4:00 pm
MEMORIAL DAY–LABOR DAY: Sun–Sat: 10:00 am–7:00 pm
CLOSED: Veteran's Day, Thanksgiving, Christmas Eve, Christmas Day, New Year's Eve, New Year's Day, Martin Luther King Jr. Day, and Presidents' Day

Golden lion tamarin (above) and red-crowned crane (below) from Bramble Park Zoo in Watertwon, SD

★ CHAHINKAPA ZOO ★

Wahpeton, North Dakota

Opened in 1933, Chahinkapa Zoo was the first zoo in North Dakota. It began with a modest collection of animals. In the late 1960s, the zoo was moved to its current location. Since then, with the help of the Chahinkapa Zoo Association, the zoo has continued to grow. In 1997, the zoo faced its most significant challenge. The zoo was flooded due to heavy rain in the Red River Valley, but all the animals were rescued and moved to higher ground. A new levee was built to protect the zoo and the town. Animal exhibits and a new petting zoo were constructed following these new protective measures.

The zoo currently features animals from six continents as well as from North Dakota. The zoo is divided into two sections, one on either side of the levee. On the east side are the hoof-stock, pheasants, and cougars, and on the west side are the orangutan, rhinoceros, and other animals. The zoo has a unique feature, its tortoise corral, where visitors can interact with several species of tortoise. All together the zoo is home to 200 animals representing about 70 species. It is accredited by the AZA and has been reaccredited each renewal since it was first accredited in 1995.

Chahinkapa Zoo is involved in many Species Survival Plans, including work with black-handed spider monkeys, fossas, and white rhinoceroses. As part of their conservation work, the zoo works hard to connect visitors to the wild animals and foster an understanding of why conservation is necessary.

Radiated tortoise from Chahinkapa Zoo in Wahpeton, ND

PLAN YOUR VISIT

ADDRESS: 1004 R.J. Hughes Drive, Wahpeton, ND 58075

MAIN PHONE: (701) 642-8709

WEBSITE: www.chahinkapazoo.org

MEMBERSHIP: www.chahinkapazoo.org/memberships

HOURS

MAY–SEPTEMBER: Sun–Sat: 10:00 am–4:00 pm

OCTOBER: Sat and Sun: 10:00 am–4:00 pm

NOVEMBER–MAY: Closed

Black-handed spider monkeys (above) and peafowl hen foster mother (below) from Chahinkapa Zoo in Wahpeton, ND

COMO PARK ZOO & CONSERVATORY

Saint Paul, Minnesota

Como Park Zoo was founded in 1897, making it one of the oldest zoos in the Midwest. It grew slowly over the years, adding a few more animals at a time. Like for so many other zoos in the Midwest, the 1930s brought significant changes to Como Park Zoo. Several new exhibits were built, and many animals were given a new home here after the Longfellow Zoo in Minneapolis closed in 1934. The next 40 years were hard on the zoo, and it was in danger of being closed several times. That all changed in 1976 with a new master plan and new commitment from the community. Since then, many new exhibits have been built, the last being the Gorilla Forest exhibit, which opened in 2013.

The zoo is home to over 1700 animals from 66 different species. Some exhibits of note are the Tropical Encounters exhibit, Gorilla Forest, Large Cat exhibit, and Polar Bear Odyssey. The bison, caribou, arctic fox, and Dall sheep are in the Old Hoof Stock Building, which is one of the oldest exhibits still in use. The zoo has been accredited by the AZA since 1986.

Como Park Zoo is involved in 46 different Species Survival Plans, including those for the emperor tamarin, lesser kudu, and polar bear. The zoo manages the studbook for crowned lemurs, which is a database of all the crowned lemurs in North America that is used to maintain genetic diversity. Another significant effort of the zoo is to encourage recycling through installing works of art made from recycled material throughout the zoo.

Dall sheep from Como Park Zoo in Saint Paul, MN

PLAN YOUR VISIT

ADDRESS: 1225 Estabrook Drive, Saint Paul, MN 55103

MAIN PHONE: (651) 487-8200

WEBSITE: www.comozooconservatory.org

MEMBERSHIP: www.comofriends.org/give/membership

HOURS

WINTER HOURS (OCTOBER–MARCH):
Sun–Sat: 10:00 am–4:00 pm

SUMMER HOURS (APRIL–SEPTEMBER):
Sun–Sat: 10:00 am–6:00 pm

Emporer tamarin (above) and lesser kudu (below) from Como Park Zoo in Saint Paul, MN

★ DAKOTA ZOO ★

Bismarck, North Dakota

Dakota Zoo opened in 1961 and was the brainchild of Marc and Betty Christianson. The zoo opened with 75 mammals and 23 birds. The zoo grew over the years, and in 1987, the zoo adopted its first master plan. The zoo has conducted three major capital campaigns since then to expand and improve animal enclosures. The latest was the "Make the Big Cats Roar" campaign, which raised $1.9 million.

The zoo is home to over 600 animals from 125 different species, and it is roughly divided between north and south. The north side is where the predators are housed, and the south side is where the ungulates mostly are. The otters and many bird species live in the center of the zoo. It has been accredited by the AZA since 1991.

The zoo is involved in several Species Survival Plans, including those for the ring-tailed lemur, snow leopard, Amur tiger, Japanese macaque, golden-headed lion tamarin, Panamanian golden frog, and red panda. In addition to this, the zoo has several other conservation and research programs. One of its significant outreach efforts is the Wild Bunch program, which is composed of staff and volunteers who work on local conservation projects in the surrounding community.

Red-tailed hawk from Dakota Zoo in Bismarck, ND

PLAN YOUR VISIT

ADDRESS: 602 Riverside Park Road, Bismarck, ND 58504

MAIN PHONE: (701) 223-7543

WEBSITE: www.dakotazoo.org

MEMBERSHIP: www.dakotazoo.org/membership

HOURS

WINTER HOURS (OCTOBER–LATE APRIL):
Fri–Sun: 1:00 pm–5:00 pm

SUMMER HOURS (LATE APRIL–SEPTEMBER):
Sun–Sat: 10:00 am–7:00 pm

North American porcupine (above) and Barbary sheep (below) from Dakota Zoo in Bismarck, ND

★ DAVID TRAYLOR ZOO OF EMPORIA ★

Emporia, Kansas

The David Traylor Zoo was founded in 1934 as Emporia Zoo. It consisted of a few deer pens, and like many other city zoos, the WPA later built a monkey island. More animals were added to the collection, and the zoo moved to its current location. Emporia Friends of the Zoo was founded in 1978 as a support organization for the zoo, and since then has raised funds for many improvements. The zoo was renamed in 2006 after David P. Traylor, who made many contributions to the zoo. In the last few years, several significant improvements have been made, and currently underway is the Oasis Campaign, the zoo's first multimillion dollar capital campaign.

The zoo is currently home to over 300 animals representing over 100 species, including lemurs, prairie dogs, and many species of birds. The zoo has added several new areas in the last few years, including the Preston Forest Adventure and Mission Madagascar. An interesting feature of the zoo is its focus on being a botanical garden, featuring pollinator gardens and landscaping features. The zoo has been accredited by the AZA since 1985.

Even as a small zoo, the David Traylor Zoo is working on several conservation projects, including the reintroduction of the black-footed ferret to Kansas. The zoo is also involved in three Species Survival Plans and a separate breeding program for alligator snapping turtles. The zoo works diligently on being a model of conservation, including efforts for rainwater collection and water reuse in the water features in the zoo.

Cape Barren goose from David Traylor Zoo in Emporia, KS

PLAN YOUR VISIT

ADDRESS: 75 Soden Road, Emporia, KS 66801
MAIN PHONE: (620) 341-4365
WEBSITE: www.emporiazoo.org
MEMBERSHIP: www.emporiazoo.org/index.php/efoz

HOURS

YEAR-ROUND: Sun–Sat: 10:00 am–4:30 pm
MEMORIAL DAY–LABOR DAY: Extended hours on Sunday and Wednesday
CLOSED: Thanksgiving, Christmas Day, and New Year's Day

Various turtles (above) and peafowl (below) from David Traylor Zoo in Emporia, KS

★ DICKERSON PARK ZOO ★

Springfield, Missouri

💬 **Dickerson Park Zoo was founded in 1923** when the city of Springfield acquired land from a former hotel that had a small private zoo. The zoo was expanded in the 1930s by the WPA, but it was largely forgotten after that and fell into disrepair. On the verge of being shut down in 1975, the zoo had new life breathed into it by the newly formed Friends of the Zoo organization. It has been completely revitalized since then into the place it is today.

🐻 **The zoo is now home to over 500 animals** from 160 different species. The zoo is divided into different areas based on continents with sections devoted to Africa, Asia, South America, North America, and Australia. The North American part has a particular focus on animals found in the state of Missouri. The zoo is in the middle of its second master plan, focusing on new exhibits and making the zoo a leader in conservation. It has been accredited by the AZA since 1986 and has been reaccredited at each renewal.

🍃 **Dickerson Park Zoo participates in several** Species Survival Plans, but their main focus is on supporting conservation and research efforts around the globe. Some of these conservation efforts include research on the maned wolf, Chacoan peccary, and red-necked ostrich. The zoo is also heavily involved in research on elephants, notably the Asian elephant.

Chacoan peccaries from Dickerson Park Zoo in Springfield, MO

PLAN YOUR VISIT

ADDRESS: 1401 W Norton Road, Springfield, MO 65803
INFO LINE: (417) 864-1800 **MAIN PHONE:** (417) 833-1570
WEBSITE: www.dickersonparkzoo.org
MEMBERSHIP: www.dickersonparkzoo.org/zoo/zoo-membership-2

HOURS

NOVEMBER–FEBRUARY: Sun–Sat: 9:00 am–4:00 pm
MARCH–OCTOBER: Sun–Sat: 9:00 am–5:00 pm
CLOSED: Thanksgiving, Christmas Day, and New Year's Day
NOTE: Closed if walkways are covered with ice or snow.

African crowned crane (above) and bongo (below) from Dickerson Park Zoo in Springfield, MO

GREAT BEND-BRIT SPAUGH ZOO

Great Bend, Kansas

Great Bend-Brit Spaugh Zoo was opened in 1953 as City Park Zoo by Brit Spaugh, the first director of public lands for the city of Great Bend. Mr. Spaugh grew and expanded the zoo until 1966 when he turned over responsibility to the next director. The zoo then began to focus on North American animals. In 1995, the third director took charge. There was a new emphasis on becoming a modern zoo and gaining accreditation. Currently, the zoo is working very hard on new enclosures and general improvements. The most recent renovation was an updated grizzly bear enclosure.

Great Bend-Brit Spaugh Zoo is home to about 180 animals from 75 different species. The zoo is small, so it is an easy walk to see all the exhibits. The zoo is home to an African leopard named Toby, grizzly bears, a mountain lion, and many smaller animals. While the zoo is not currently accredited, it does maintain accreditation standards in animal care.

The zoo's main conservation effort is its Raptor Center. It focuses on rehabilitation and habitat preservation, along with research and education. The zoo is involved in nine Species Survival Programs, including that for the red-legged seriema.

Red-legged seriema from Great Bend-Brit Spaugh Zoo in Great Bend, KS

PLAN YOUR VISIT

ADDRESS: 2123 Main Street, Great Bend, KS 67530

MAIN PHONE: (620) 793-4226

WEBSITE: www.greatbendzoo.com

MEMBERSHIP: www.greatbendks.net/306/Zoo-Society

HOURS

YEAR-ROUND: Sun–Sat: 9:00 am–3:00 pm

CLOSED: Thanksgiving and Christmas Day

Grivet monkey (above) and African leopard (below) from Great Bend-Brit Spaugh Zoo in Great Bend, KS

★ GREAT PLAINS ZOO ★

Sioux Falls, South Dakota

Great Plains Zoo formally opened in 1963, but its history goes back to 1931. That year Sioux Falls took over a collection of animals, placing them on display in Sherman Park. The zoo grew over the intervening years, moving to its current location in 1963. Despite some rough years in the early 2000s, the zoo has improved each year and is a major attraction in South Dakota. It is owned by the city and operated by the Zoological Society of Sioux Falls, a non-profit that manages the zoo.

The zoo has several distinct areas, including Asian Cats, Face-to-Face Farm, African Savannah, Primates, and the Fortress of the Bears. The zoo has an award-winning Japanese macaques exhibit.

All in all, the zoo is home to over 1000 animals from 137 species. The zoo is accredited by the AZA and recently was awarded a Quarter Century Award. Also at the zoo is the Delbridge Museum of Natural History, which has an impressive collection of over 150 mounted animals, including 38 critically endangered species.

Great Plains Zoo participates in 43 different Species Survival Plans, including those for the Amur tiger, Japanese macaque, and snow leopard. In addition, it supports conservation efforts locally and abroad, including pollinator projects in Minnesota and South Dakota, rhinoceros research in Namibia, and a raptor rehabilitation center.

African spurred tortoise from Great Plains Zoo in Sioux Falls, SD

PLAN YOUR VISIT

ADDRESS: 805 S Kiwanis Avenue, Sioux Falls, SD 57104

MAIN PHONE: (605) 367-7003

WEBSITE: www.greatzoo.org

MEMBERSHIP: www.greatzoo.org/membership

HOURS

MEMORIAL DAY–LABOR DAY: Mon–Sat: 9:00 am–7:00 pm & Sun: 11:00 am–7:00 pm

SEPTEMBER: Mon–Sat: 10:00 am–6:00 pm & Sun: 11:00 am–6:00 pm

OCTOBER–MARCH: Mon–Sat: 10:00 am–5:00 pm & Sun: 11:00 am–5:00 pm

CLOSED: Thanksgiving, Christmas Eve, Christmas Day, and New Year's Day

Chinese alligator (above) and kookaburra (below) from Great Plains Zoo in Sioux Falls, SD

★ HEMKER PARK & ZOO ★

Freeport, Minnesota

Hemker Park and Zoo officially opened to the public in 1994 as Hemker Wildlife Park. It is a private family-run zoo and one of the few that is accredited. The zoo began as the dream of Mark and Joan Hemker and has grown steadily since the couple adopted their first animals in 1977. In 2006, Mark passed away, and the family has continued to operate the zoo in his honor. In 2008, they added a petting zoo and picnic area and renamed the zoo, giving it its current name.

Hemker Park and Zoo is very easy to navigate. The main area is a big walking loop around the hoofstock enclosures. Near the entrance are several enclosures, including the one for red pandas. At the back of the loop are the waterfowl and otters. And just past the waterfowl is the farmyard, with goats and alpacas. All in all, the zoo is home to over 300 animals from 60 different species. The zoo is accredited by the Zoological Association of America (ZAA).

The zoo works with numerous breeding programs for endangered species at the zoo. In addition to these conservation efforts, the zoo participates in several conservation programs across the globe. These programs include efforts on behalf of African black-footed penguins and red-legged seriemas. The zoo's latest endeavor is a new non-profit called Guardians of Conservation. Its mission is to raise funds for the zoo and its conservation work at home and abroad.

Sitatungas from Hemker Park and Zoo in Freeport, MN

PLAN YOUR VISIT

ADDRESS: 26715 County Road 39, Freeport, MN 56331

MAIN PHONE: (320) 836-2426

WEBSITE: www.hemkerzoo.com

FOUNDATION: www.hemkerzoo.com/product/
guardians-of-conservation-donation

HOURS

MAY–OCTOBER: Sun–Sat: 10:00 am–6:00 pm

NOVEMBER–APRIL: Closed

Transcaspian urial shedding her coat and male bontebok (above) and great horned owl (below) from Hemker Park and Zoo in Freeport, MN

★ HENRY DOORLY ZOO & AQUARIUM ★

Omaha, Nebraska

Henry Doorly Zoo and Aquarium was founded in 1894 as Riverview Park Zoo. In 1898, the zoo had about 120 animals, including a menagerie on loan from William "Buffalo Bill" Cody. After a significant donation in 1952, the zoo was renamed Henry Doorly Zoo. The zoo continued to expand over the years and added many all-season exhibits like the indoor rainforest called Lied Jungle and indoor desert called Desert Dome. Today the zoo is a world leader in conservation and has received numerous awards for their conservation work.

The zoo is organized into eight main areas: Lied Jungle, Scott Aquarium, Desert Dome, African Grasslands, Asian Highlands, Hubbard Great Ape Complex, Big Cat Complex, and the Children's Adventure Trails. Many of the exhibits are indoors, allowing visitors to come year-round.

One of these is the Desert Dome, which lets visitors experience many different desert biomes from around the world. The Desert Dome also houses Kingdoms of the Night, one of the most extensive nocturnal exhibits in the world. The zoo is home to over 17,000 animals from 962 species and covers over 130 acres of land. The zoo is accredited by the AZA.

The zoo is involved in several Species Survival Plans, including those for the Amur tiger, lowland gorilla, okapi, and snow leopard. The zoo also has a state-of-the-art research center near the center of the grounds. The facility is nearly 30,000 square feet and has research labs, an animal nursery, and veterinary medical facilities. The research being conducted there helps both zoos and conservation efforts in the wild.

Roadrunner from Henry Doorly Zoo in Omaha, NE

PLAN YOUR VISIT

ADDRESS: 3701 S 10th Street, Omaha, NE 68107

INFO LINE: (402) 733-8400

MAIN PHONE: (402) 733-8401

WEBSITE: www.omahazoo.com

MEMBERSHIP: www.omahazoo.com/become-a-member

HOURS

APRIL–OCTOBER: Sun–Sat: 9:00 am–5:00 pm

NOVEMBER–MARCH: Sun–Sat: 10:00 am–4:00 pm

CLOSED: Christmas Day

NOTE: Buildings remain open one hour after close.

Klipspringer (above) and Cape thick-knee (below) from Henry Doorly Zoo in Omaha, NE

★ HUTCHINSON ZOO ★

Hutchinson, Kansas

💬 **Hutchinson Zoo is one of the newer zoos in** the Midwest. It opened its doors in 1986 after a year of work by the Hutchinson Friends of the Zoo. It began with a petting zoo, Wild Habitats building, and play area. Over the years, the zoo expanded to include a prairie dog enclosure and a wildlife rehabilitation center. Hutchinson Zoo suffered a significant setback in 2007 when flooding covered much of the zoo, but it has bounced back and is now better than ever. The zoo continues to grow, adding new animals to the collection.

🐻 **Hutchinson Zoo is one of the smaller accred-** ited zoos in the Midwest. The zoo has several themed areas, including Staying Alive, featuring animals that live alongside people, and Animals and Man, which is a petting zoo. These two areas were some of the first exhibits at the zoo. The zoo has been accredited by the AZA since 1997.

🍃 **The zoo is involved in several Species Sur-** vival Plans, most importantly that for the black-footed ferret, one of North America's most endangered species. The zoo is home to the Cargill Wildcare Center, a wildlife rehabilitation facility. The center treats over 500 injured animals a year, nursing them back to health and releasing them back into the wild if possible.

Burrowing owl from Hutchinson Zoo in Hutchinson, KS

PLAN YOUR VISIT

ADDRESS: 6 Emerson Loop E, Hutchinson, KS 67501
INFO LINE: (620) 694-2693
WEBSITE: www.hutchinsonzoo.org
MEMBERSHIP: www.hutchinsonzoo.org/168/
    Zoo-Memberships

HOURS

YEAR-ROUND: Sun–Sat: 10:00 am–4:45 pm
CLOSED: Thanksgiving, Christmas Day, and
    New Year's Day

Little blue heron (above) and dwarf caimans (below) from Hutchinson Zoo in Hutchinson, KS

★ KANSAS CITY ZOO ★

Kansas City, Missouri

The Kansas City Zoo opened in 1909 with a handful of animals. The zoo gradually grew over the years, adding a petting zoo and other facilities. In 2002, the management of the zoo was turned over to the non-profit Friends of the Zoo. This was a turning point for the institution. After an extensive capital campaign lasting several years, the zoo was transformed into the place it is today. The zoo now covers 202 acres and has many high-quality enclosures.

The zoo features five themed base areas: East Africa, West Africa, Australia, Tiger Trail, and KidZone. An older area once called The Valley was retired in 2005. However, the area still has many exhibits that are still in use. One of the more impressive areas is the one dedicated to East Africa. It is home to a large pasture area housing five species of antelope, zebras, and giraffes. This area also houses an expansive chimpanzee exhibit. The zoo is home to over 1300 animals and is accredited by the AZA.

The zoo is involved in several Species Survival Plans, including those for the Bornean orangutan, two-toed sloth, tree kangaroo, and cheetah. It also participates in several research and conservation programs outside of the zoo, such as for the trumpeter swan and Wyoming toad reintroduction. The zoo is involved in several field conservation programs as well, like the Humboldt penguin conservation effort and the Polar Bear Research Project.

African ground hornbill from Kansas City Zoo in Kansas City, MO

PLAN YOUR VISIT

ADDRESS: 6800 Zoo Drive, Kansas City, MO 64110
MAIN PHONE: (816) 595-1234
WEBSITE: www.kansascityzoo.org
MEMBERSHIP: www.kansascityzoo.org/visitor-info/ membership

HOURS

NOVEMBER–FEBRUARY: Sun–Sat: 9:30 am–4:00 pm
MEMORIAL DAY–LABOR DAY: Mon–Fri: 8:00 am–4:00 pm & Sat–Sun: 8:00 am–5:00 pm
MARCH–MAY, SEPTEMBER–OCTOBER: Mon–Fri: 9:30 am–4:00 pm & Sat–Sun: 9:30 am–5:00 pm
CLOSED: Thanksgiving, Christmas Day, and New Year's Day

Scimitar-horned oryx (above) and rock hyrax (below) from Kansas City Zoo in Kansas City, MO

★ LAKE SUPERIOR ZOO ★

Duluth, Minnesota

💬 **Lake Superior Zoo was opened by Bert Onsgard in 1923.** Originally named Duluth Zoo, it started with a small number of exhibits. Over the years the zoo has been home to a variety of animals, including Valerie, a Himalayan black bear who flew as a mascot on bombing missions in World War II. The zoo was first accredited in 1985 with its increasing emphasis on conservation, animal welfare, and education and was renamed Lake Superior Zoo in 1987. The zoo fell on hard times in the late 2000s, but management of the zoo was turned over to the Lake Superior Zoological Society in 2009 and since then, the zoo has completed multiple projects, including a new bear exhibit in 2019.

🐻 **The zoo is organized by region of the world,** with areas devoted to Asia and Australia. There are other areas dedicated specifically to primates, nocturnal animals, and a petting zoo. The redesigned main building includes many exhibits devoted to birds and reptiles. As of 2017, the zoo is home to over 400 animals representing 131 different species with that number growing each year. The zoo was first accredited by the AZA in 1985 and remained so except for a brief five-year period from 2006 to 2011.

🦡 **Lake Superior Zoo is involved in 30 different** Species Survival Plans, including those for the brush-tailed bettong, Amur tiger, and swift fox. The zoo works on projects around the world by raising money for the likes of the Peregrine Fund, saving California condors, and the Alala Project, which reintroduces Hawaiian crows into the wild. Locally, it has several conservation projects and fundraisers.

Brush-tailed bettong from Lake Superior Zoo in Duluth, MN

PLAN YOUR VISIT

ADDRESS: 7210 Fremont Street, Duluth, MN 55807

MAIN PHONE: (218) 730-4500

WEBSITE: www.lszooduluth.org

MEMBERSHIP: www.lszooduluth.org/membership

HOURS

MEMORIAL DAY–LABOR DAY: Sun–Sat: 10:00 am–5:00 pm

LABOR DAY–MEMORIAL DAY: Sun–Sat: 10:00 am–4:00 pm

CLOSED: Thanksgiving, Christmas Day, New Year's Day, and closes at 1:00 pm on Christmas Eve

Bobwhite (above) and Burmese python (below) from Lake Superior Zoo in Duluth, MN

★ LEE G. SIMMONS CONSERVATION ★ PARK & WILDLIFE SAFARI

Ashland, Nebraska

The Lee G. Simmons Conservation Park and Wildlife Safari, an extension of the nearby Henry Doorly Zoo in Omaha, was opened in 1998. The park focuses on animals from North America in a drive-through safari-type setting. It has grown in the intervening years, adding a bald eagle aviary in 2010 and the Crane Meadows Viewing Tower in 2013. However, most of the work done in the park is off-limits to regular visitors. It serves as the winter home for some of the animals from the zoo in Omaha and is home to cheetah and tiger breeding programs.

The park is primarily a drive-through experience with visitors passing through Elk Prairie, Crane Meadows, and finally Bison Plains in their cars. The middle of the park has a parking area where visitors can leave their cars behind and visit the petting zoo, Eagle Aviary, and Wolf Canyon. Separate from the zoo, the park has its own accreditation from the AZA.

The real conservation work at this park goes on behind the scenes and away from the public eye. It runs a cheetah breeding facility, a four-acre complex that can house up to 12 cheetahs. The park is also working on a second facility especially for tigers. Situated on five acres, this new facility will allow for six tigers to be housed at a time. By having these behind-the-scenes locations, the park can more carefully control the breeding process and have more successful matings.

Bald eagle from Lee G. Simmons Wildlife Safari Park in Ashland, NE

PLAN YOUR VISIT

ADDRESS: 16406 N 292 Street, Ashland, NE 68003

INFO LINE: (402) 944-WILD (9453)

WEBSITE: www.wildlifesafaripark.com

MEMBERSHIP: www.wildlifesafaripark.com/memberships

HOURS

APRIL–OCTOBER: Sun–Sat: 9:00 am–5:00 pm

OCTOBER–APRIL: Closed

NOTE: Call or check the website for actual dates for the season.

North American elk (above) and sandhill crane (below) from Lee G. Simmons Wildlife Safari Park in Ashland, NE

★ LEE RICHARDSON ZOO ★

Garden City, Kansas

The Lee Richardson Zoo was founded in 1927 as Garden City Zoo by the local chapter of the Izaak Walton League. The original plan was to house animals native to the area. Over time, the collection grew in size and broadened in scope. The zoo was renamed in 1950 after the founder and first superintendent, Lee Richardson. The zoo continued to grow over the intervening years, adding new areas and additional animals.

The zoo is currently home to over 500 animals representing over 100 species, including bison, giraffes, and rhinos. The zoo is divided into several areas, with its most notable sections devoted to the North American Plains, Cat Canyon, and Wild Asia. The latest project is a new primate habitat, which it is raising funds to build. There is also a way to drive through the zoo for a small fee, but pedestrians are admitted for free. The zoo has been accredited by the AZA since 1986.

Lee Richardson Zoo is actively involved in many Species Survival Plans, including those for the snow leopard, Chinese goral, and sloth bear. The zoo also participates in the statewide program to reintroduce the black-footed ferret in conjunction with other zoos in Kansas. The zoo raises funds for conservation efforts around the world, including the Sahara Conservation Fund and Amphibian Ark Project. Locally, the zoo offers several educational opportunities and supports local efforts to save the monarch butterfly.

Sloth bear from Lee Richardson Zoo in Garden City, KS

PLAN YOUR VISIT

ADDRESS: 312 E Finnup Drive, Garden City, KS 67846

MAIN PHONE: (620) 276-1250

WEBSITE: www.leerichardsonzoo.org

MEMBERSHIP: www.leerichardsonzoo.org/become-a-zoo-member

HOURS

APRIL–LABOR DAY: Sun–Sat: 8:00 am–7:00 pm

LABOR DAY–MARCH: Sun–Sat: 8:00 am–5:00 pm

CLOSED: Thanksgiving, Christmas Day, and New Year's Day

Patagonian cavies (above) and banteng (below) from Lee Richardson Zoo in Garden City, KS

★ LINCOLN CHILDREN'S ZOO ★

Lincoln, Nebraska

In 1959, Arnott Folsom began planning for a children's zoo using his own money. By the summer of 1963, the zoo was under construction, and one of the first projects completed was the railroad. Mr. Folsom opened the railroad and sold 150,000 tickets, which helped to finish funding the zoo. The zoo opened seasonally in 1964 and full time in 1973. The zoo has been growing ever since but has remained true to its original mission of being a children's zoo. The latest additions to the zoo were giraffes, tigers, and red pandas.

The zoo has many areas dedicated to children, including the Secret Jungle where kids can climb around alongside spider monkeys, the Stego Dino Dig area where they can dig bones out of the sand, and a nice animal petting area. The zoo is home to over 400 animals from over 100 different species, and it is accredited by the AZA.

The zoo participates in many Species Survival Plans, including those for the fossa, red panda, and snow leopard. In addition, the zoo is home to the Red Panda Conservation Center, which is dedicated to better understanding the red panda and saving them from extinction. Another important project of the zoo is its collaboration with Joel Satore on his Photo Ark project, which began there.

Red-rumped agouti from Lincoln Children's Zoo in Lincoln, NE

PLAN YOUR VISIT

ADDRESS: 222 S 27th Street, Lincoln, NE 68502

MAIN PHONE: (402) 475-6741

WEBSITE: www.lincolnzoo.org

MEMBERSHIP: www.lincolnzoo.org/membership

HOURS

YEAR-ROUND: Sun–Sat: 10:00 am–5:00 pm

CLOSED: Thanksgiving, Christmas Eve, Christmas Day, New Year's Eve, and New Year's Day

Clouded leopard (above) and Prevost's squirrel (below) from Lincoln Children's Zoo in Lincoln, NE

★ MINNESOTA ZOO ★

Apple Valley, Minnesota

💬 **The Minnesota Zoo opened in May of 1978,** making it one of the younger zoos in the Midwest. Because it was opened in a rural area outside of Minneapolis, it was able to build expansive exhibits from the start. The zoo is one of only two zoos in the United States that is operated by a state government and not by a local organization or municipality.

🐻 **The zoo is home to over 4990 animals from** over 533 species. Ever since its founding, the zoo grounds have been organized by habitat and not by species. There are seven themed habitat areas in total: Medtronic Minnesota Trail, Northern Trail, Tropics Trail, Discovery Bay, Russia's Grizzly Coast,

Wells Fargo Family Farm, and an Australian area inside the Northern Trail area. There are plans to split the Northern Trail area into two additional areas, featuring the Mongolian Steppes and Edge of the Himalayas. Altogether, the zoo covers 485 acres. The zoo is accredited by the AZA.

🍃 **The zoo participates in conservation efforts** for several species, including for the dhole, Asian wild dog, and Przewalski's horse. It is also active in many conservation efforts at home and around the world, including efforts to save the Amur leopard and Amur tiger from extinction. The zoo has won numerous awards, particularly for its work with tigers.

Dhole from Minnesota Zoo in Apple Valley, MN

PLAN YOUR VISIT

ADDRESS: 13000 Zoo Boulevard, Apple Valley, MN 55124

INFO LINE: (952) 431-9500

WEBSITE: www.mnzoo.org

MEMBERSHIP: www.mnzoo.org/get-involved/
   membership

HOURS

MAY AND SEPTEMBER: Mon–Fri: 9:00 am–4:00 pm &
   Sat–Sun: 9:00 am–6:00 pm

MEMORIAL DAY–LABOR DAY: Sun–Sat: 9:00 am–6:00 pm

OCTOBER–APRIL: Sun–Sat: 9:00 am–4:00 pm

CLOSED: Thanksgiving and Christmas Day

Moose (above) and Komodo dragon (below) from Minnesota Zoo in Apple Valley, MN

★ RED RIVER ZOO ★

Fargo, North Dakota

Red River Zoo is the newest zoo in the Midwest, having opened its doors in 1999. The zoo started small with only eight acres of land, which was part of a more substantial donation of an old farm called Red River Ranch. The zoo has grown steadily since then, adding exhibits and creating a landscape with hills on the once flat piece of land. The zoo focuses on species that live in climates similar to North Dakota's and has animals from around the world.

The zoo is home to over 800 animals from over 89 different species. It features many excellent exhibits, including an exhibit for a family of gray wolves that can be seen from outside or inside the Trapper's Cabin and a very well-done otter exhibit. One of the more interesting features of the zoo is the Children's Zoo Farm, which features different kinds of crops in addition to the animals on display. The zoo has been accredited by the AZA since 2006.

The zoo participates in conservation efforts for several species, including for the red panda, Pallas's cat, and white-naped crane. It is one of the most successful zoos in the world in the breeding of red pandas and Pallas's cats. In fact, in 2013 the zoo received the Edward H. Bean Award for its work with red pandas.

Northern blue-tongued skink from Red River Zoo in Fargo, ND

PLAN YOUR VISIT

ADDRESS: 4255 23rd Avenue S, Fargo, ND 58104

MAIN PHONE: (701) 277-9240

WEBSITE: www.redriverzoo.org

MEMBERSHIP: redriverzoo.org/membership-overview

HOURS

SUMMER: Sun–Sat: 10:00 am–7:00 pm

FALL AND WINTER: Sun–Sat: 10:00 am–5:00 pm

Pallas's cat (above) and red-breasted goose (below) from Red River Zoo in Fargo, ND

RIVERSIDE DISCOVERY CENTER

Scottsbluff, Nebraska

Established in 1950 as Riverside Zoo, it opened as many small zoos did with a small herd of deer and some waterfowl. The zoo grew slowly over the years until the late 1980s and early 1990s, which saw major renovations and upgrades. It was in this same time frame that the first of two fundraising organizations for the zoo, Riverside Zoological Society, was created. In later years, the zoo merged with two other organizations to become Riverside Discovery Center.

Riverside Discovery Center is home to over 200 animals from over 70 different species. The zoo is designed to be kid-friendly. In addition to the exhibits, it has several play areas scattered throughout the complex. The animal enclosures are split into small zones, including the Rainforest Discovery Center, Cat Complex, and Primate Building. The zoo has been accredited by the AZA since 1990.

The zoo is involved in 16 Species Survival Plans, ranging from those for Amur tigers to chimpanzees to swift foxes. Aside from these efforts, the zoo also raises money for several conservation efforts at home and abroad. Riverside Discovery Center holds several events for the local community to raise awareness about conservation issues, including the Conservation Carnival held each August. It also offers many educational opportunities to learn more about conservation, especially for local schools.

Muntjac from Riverside Discovery Center in Scottsbluff, NE

PLAN YOUR VISIT

ADDRESS: 1600 S Beltline Hwy W, Scottsbluff, NE 69361

MAIN PHONE: (308) 630-6236

WEBSITE: www.riversidediscoverycenter.org

MEMBERSHIP: www.riversidediscoverycenter.org/ membership

HOURS

SUMMER: Sun–Sat: 9:30 am–4:00 pm

WINTER: Sun–Sat: 10:00 am–4:00 pm

Peafowl male (above) and swift fox (below) from Riverside Discovery Center in Scottsbluff, NE

★ ROLLING HILLS ZOO ★

Salina, Kansas

💬 **Charlie Walker purchased land for a ranch,** called Rolling Hills Ranch, in the early 1980s. It was soon a regular visit for schoolchildren to learn about the draft horses he kept. Not long after that, he added some additional animals, like bears and a lioness. In 1995, the exotic animal portion of the ranch was broken off as its own non-profit organization, and land and equipment were donated to build a zoo. Rolling Hills Zoo opened to the public in the fall of 1999. In 2005, a wildlife museum was added to showcase other animals the zoo did not have.

🐻 **Rolling Hills Zoo is one of two zoos in the** Midwest that also have a natural history museum, the other being Great Plains Zoo in South Dakota. The zoo itself is home to over 390 animals from over 120 different species. The zoo features a large rhino barn, which also houses some of the primates over the winter, and several themed areas that showcase big cats and apes. The zoo was accredited by the AZA even before it opened to the public.

🍃 **Rolling Hills Zoo, like the other accredited** zoos in Kansas, is working on the ornate box turtle project and the reintroduction of the black-footed ferret to Kansas. In addition, it is active in all the Species Survival Plans for the animals under its care, including those for the coatimundi, addax, and African wild dog.

White rhinoceros from Rolling Hills Zoo in Salina, KS

PLAN YOUR VISIT

ADDRESS: 625 N Hedville Road, Salina, KS 67401

MAIN PHONE: (785) 827-9488

WEBSITE: www.rollinghillszoo.org

MEMBERSHIP: www.rollinghillszoo.org/membership

HOURS

PEAK SEASON: Sun–Sat: 9:00 am–5:00 pm

OFF-SEASON: Sun–Sat: 9:00 am–4:00 pm

CLOSED: Thanksgiving, Christmas Eve, Christmas Day and New Year's Day

NOTE: Peak season coincides with daylight savings time.

Quince monitor (above) and capybara (below) from Rolling Hills Zoo in Salina, KS

★ ROOSEVELT PARK ZOO ★

Minot, North Dakota

Roosevelt Park Zoo opened in 1920 with a single bison. The next year the zoo added a couple of bear cubs and a zoo building. It grew steadily over the years until 1969 when tragedy struck the zoo. The zoo grounds were completely flooded. But this was a blessing in disguise as it allowed the zoo to rebuild almost from scratch. The following year, the zoo separated from the rest of the park and has been growing steadily ever since. That same year, the Greater Minot Zoological Society was founded to help build new enclosures for the big cats. In 2011, the unthinkable happened—the zoo was flooded again. The zoo remained closed for almost two years, but once again, it was able to be rebuilt into an even better zoo than before.

Roosevelt Park Zoo is divided in half by the Souris River. The central part of the zoo is home to the big cats, hoofstock from around the world, and the zoo's aviary. The second part of the zoo is accessible by a bridge over the river. This area is home to mostly North American animals, the Discovery Barn, and the children's zoo. All in all, the zoo is home to over 200 animals from over 65 different species. It has been accredited by the AZA since 1989.

The zoo participates in 27 different Species Survival Plans, including those for the snow leopard, Kirk's dik-dik, and Japanese serow. It also raises funds for conservation programs around the world. Last fiscal year, the zoo raised over $22,000 that went to programs like the Okapi Conservation Foundation and Giraffe Conservation Alliance.

Warthog from Roosevelt Park Zoo in Minot, ND

PLAN YOUR VISIT

ADDRESS: 1219 Burdick Expressway E,
Minot, ND 58701

MAIN PHONE: (701) 857-4166

WEBSITE: www.rpzoo.com

MEMBERSHIP: www.rpzoo.com/memberships

HOURS

MAY AND SEPTEMBER: Sun–Sat: 10:00 am–6:00 pm

JUNE–AUGUST: Sun–Sat: 10:00 am–8:00 pm

OCTOBER–APRIL: Mon–Sat: 10:00 am–3:00 pm

CLOSED: Thanksgiving and Christmas Day

Japanese serow (above) and Kirk's dik-dik (below) from Roosevelt Park Zoo in Minot, ND

★ SAINT LOUIS ZOO ★

Saint Louis, Missouri

💬 **The Saint Louis Zoo was founded in 1910.** The first exhibit, a large walk-through birdcage, was purchased six years before that in 1904 after the World's Fair. In 1921, the zoo built the Bear Pits, which was considered a model enclosure at the time. The zoo has continued to create high-quality exhibits over the years. In 2010, the zoo embarked on a significant capital campaign to improve zoo facilities leading to the building of several new exhibits. One of the more unique things about the zoo is that it is free of charge due to the generosity of Saint Louis taxpayers.

🐻 **The zoo is divided into six areas: Lakeside** Crossing, River's Edge, Discovery Corner, the Wild, Historic Hill, and Red Rocks. Each area has many animals from different regions of the world. One of the more fascinating areas is Historic Hill. This was one of the core areas of the original zoo and is home to the 1904 Flight Cage, which is still in use. It is also home to the Bird House and Herpetarium. The zoo is accredited by the AZA and is home to over 16,000 animals and many endangered species.

🍃 **The zoo is involved in several Species Survival Plans,** including those for the Grevy's zebra, Somali wild ass, okapi, and black-and-white colobus monkey. The zoo is also home to the Institute for Conservation Medicine. The research being conducted there focuses on a holistic approach to wildlife conservation, public health, and sustainable ecosystems.

Babirusa from Saint Louis Zoo in Saint Louis, MO

PLAN YOUR VISIT

ADDRESS: One Government Drive, Saint Louis, MO 63110

MAIN PHONE: (314) 781-0900

WEBSITE: www.stlzoo.org

MEMBERSHIP: www.stlzoo.org/membership

HOURS

SPRING & FALL: Sun–Sat: 9:00 am–5:00 pm

SUMMER: Sun–Thu: 8:00 am–5:00 pm & Fri–Sat: 8:00 am–7:00 pm

WINTER: Sun–Sat: 9:00 am–4:00 pm

CLOSED: Christmas Day and New Year's Day

Butterfly (above) and fennec fox (below) from Saint Louis Zoo in Saint Louis, MO

★ SEDGWICK COUNTY ZOO ★

Wichita, Kansas

💬 **The Sedgwick County Zoo was founded in** 1971 through a partnership between Sedgwick County and the Sedgwick County Zoological Society. It is the largest zoo in Kansas and one of the largest zoos in the country. Initially, it opened with just two areas, but it has grown and expanded over the years. Two recent additions include the Slawson Family Tiger Trek and Downing Gorilla Forest. The zoo is currently working on a 25-year master plan, which provides for significant overhauls and expansions.

🐻 **The zoo is roughly divided by continent,** with areas for Asia, Africa, South America, and Australia. In addition, it also has several specialty areas like the Tiger Trek and Gorilla Forest. In total, the zoo is home to over 3000 animals representing nearly 400 species. It is nationally recognized for its excellent exhibits and successful breeding of endangered species. The zoo is accredited by the AZA.

🌿 **Sedgwick County Zoo is involved in many** Species Survival Plans, including those for the jaguar, African elephant, and Burmese brow-antlered deer. One interesting conservation program the zoo works on outside of these programs is with the Livestock Conservancy. This program works to save endangered breeds of domestic livestock from extinction. On the local level, the zoo is involved in the black-footed ferret reintroduction project and has several community outreach programs.

Broad-snouted caiman from Sedgwick County Zoo in Wichita, KS

PLAN YOUR VISIT

ADDRESS: 5555 W Zoo Boulevard, Wichita, KS 67212

MAIN PHONE: (316) 660-9453

WEBSITE: www.scz.org

MEMBERSHIP: www.scz.org/membership

HOURS

YEAR-ROUND: Sun–Sat: 9:00 am–5:00 pm

CLOSED: The first Saturday after Labor Day

Southern pudu (above) and Burmese brow-antlered deer (below) from Sedgwick County Zoo in Wichita, KS

★ SUNSET ZOO ★

Manhattan, Kansas

💬 **In 1929, the city of Manhattan purchased a** plot of land called Sunset Cemetery. In the areas that were too hilly or rocky, the city began work on a zoo. It was officially chartered in 1934 as a park. The WPA was instrumental in providing the early funding for the zoo, and much of the original limestone work from then has been preserved and included in the zoo's master plan. In 1980, the city began charging admission and using the proceeds to modernize and expand the zoo. One of the more recent projects, the John Woodard Memorial Gibbons Exhibit, featured some of the zoo's original limestone work.

🐻 **Sunset Zoo has five main areas: three trails** dedicated to Africa, Asia, and South America; the Australian Walkabout area; and the Kansas Plains area. One of the more interesting exhibits is the maned wolf and giant anteater enclosure. The animals live together just as they might on the South American savanna. The zoo is accredited by the AZA and has been since 1989.

🍃 **The zoo is involved with many conservation** efforts at home and around the world. In particular, it has partnered with Wildlife SOS, a non-profit in India, to support sloth bears, and also has several projects in Paraguay. Locally, the zoo has worked on black-footed ferret reintroduction and with a local beekeepers' association. It is also active in many Species Survival Plans, including those for the Asian small-clawed otter and red-crowned crane.

Bolivian reed titi monkey from Sunset Zoo in Manhattan, KS

PLAN YOUR VISIT

ADDRESS: 2333 Oak Street, Manhattan, KS 66502

MAIN PHONE: (785) 587-2737

WEBSITE: www.sunsetzoo.com

MEMBERSHIP: www.sunsetzoo.com/149/Become-a-FOSZ-Member

HOURS

APRIL–OCTOBER: Sun–Sat: 9:30 am–5:00 pm

NOVEMBER–MARCH: Sun–Sat: 12:00 pm–5:00 pm

CLOSED: Thanksgiving, the Friday after Thanksgiving, Christmas Eve, Christmas Day, and New Year's Day

Asian small-clawed otters (above) and red-crowned crane (below) from Sunset Zoo in Manhattan, KS

★ TANGANYIKA WILDLIFE PARK ★

Goddard, Kansas

Jim Fouts began work on what would become Tanganyika Wildlife Park in 1985. It is one of only two privately run and accredited zoos in the Midwest, the other being Hemker Park and Zoo in Minnesota. In 1987, the park expanded to house tigers, and by 2000, private tours were being given of the facilities containing a mere seven species. The park officially opened to the public in 2008 with 15 exhibits. It has grown over the intervening years and now has 40 exhibits and 10 interactive stations.

The park is home to over 400 animals representing over 45 different species. It features numerous interactive stations where visitors can feed various animals. The park is small enough to be an easy walk for most visitors. Some notable exhibits include snow leopards, okapis, and pygmy hippopotamuses. The zoo is accredited by the ZAA.

Tanganyika Wildlife Park supports numerous conservation programs in the wild, including those for rhinos, African carnivores, and gibbons in Asia. Also, it is a very successful breeder of endangered species, particularly of big cats.

Lorikeet from Tanganyika Wildlife Park in Goddard, KS

PLAN YOUR VISIT

ADDRESS: 1000 S Hawkins Lane, Goddard, KS 67052

MAIN PHONE: (316) 794-8954

WEBSITE: www.twpark.com

SEASON PASS: www.twpark.com/seasonpass

HOURS

MARCH–APRIL: Sun–Sat: 10:00 am–4:00 pm

MAY–LABOR DAY: Sun–Sat: 9:00 am–5:00 pm

LABOR DAY–OCTOBER: Sun–Sat: 10:00 am–4:00 pm

NOVEMBER–MARCH: Closed

NOTE: Call or check the website for actual closing and opening dates.

Sulcata tortoise (above) and binturong (below) from Tanganyika Wildlife Park in Goddard, KS

TOPEKA ZOO & CONSERVATION CENTER

Topeka, Kansas

The park where the Topeka Zoo is located was opened in 1899 when the Gage family made a donation of land to the city of Topeka. Later, in 1933, the zoo opened its doors, growing steadily over the years. In 1963, Gary Clarke was named the first zoo director. Under his leadership the zoo blossomed and became a major attraction. After his retirement, the zoo fell on hard times, but in 2003, it was given a major overhaul and became the place it is today.

The Topeka Zoo features one of the first indoor rain forests ever built in the United States, which opened in 1974. The zoo also has other areas of note, including Hill's Black Bear Woods, home to the zoo's black bears, and the Animals and Man building, which is the indoor home of the hippopotamuses, elephants, and giraffes. The zoo is home to over 300 animals representing over 110 species and has been continually accredited by the AZA since 2003.

The zoo participates in over 35 Species Survival Plans, including those for the patas monkey, Nicobar pigeon, and greater Malayan chevrotain. In addition, the zoo is working with the other accredited zoos in Kansas to survey the ornate box turtle population, which is the state reptile of Kansas. It also holds educational sessions in the community about the monarch butterfly and what people can do to help prevent it from dying off by planting pollinator gardens.

Greater Malayan chevrotain from Topeka Zoo in Topeka, KS

PLAN YOUR VISIT

ADDRESS: 635 SW Gage Boulevard, Topeka, KS 66606

INFO LINE: (785) 368-9140

WEBSITE: www.topekazoo.org

MEMBERSHIP: www.topekazoo.org/membership

HOURS

YEAR-ROUND: Sun–Sat: 9:00 am–4:30 pm

CLOSED: Veteran's Day, Thanksgiving, Christmas Day, and New Year's Day

NOTE: The zoo remains open until 5:00 pm even though the last admission is at 4:30 pm.

Patas monkeys (above) and Nicobar pigeon (below) from Topeka Zoo in Topeka, KS

★ WRIGHT PARK ZOO ★

Dodge City, Kansas

Wright Park in Dodge City has had animals since before 1926. In that year, a pair of African lions were acquired to go with the black bears and raccoons already on exhibit in the park. It continued to grow over the years, adding bison, deer, and monkeys. Wright Park Zoo took its current form in the mid- to late-1980s. The zoo went through a major renovation during this time, upgrading to brand-new, modern exhibits for the animals. The zoo is currently working on fundraising for a new master plan. This plan would completely overhaul the zoo, adding exhibits and upgrading and improving the current exhibits.

The zoo is currently home to over 120 animals representing over 30 species, including bison, gray wolves, and a bobcat. The zoo is small, covering just four acres of the large park. One of the more interesting exhibits is a walk-through aviary, which houses many birds from across the globe. The zoo has been accredited by the ZAA since 2010.

Being a very small zoo with a small staff, the zoo does not participate in Species Survival Plans at the moment. However, it would like to do so once it accomplishes some of the work that is part of the new master plan. This plan will provide some of the upgraded facilities necessary to be involved in more conservation work.

Texas Longhorn cow from Wright Park Zoo in Dodge City, KS

PLAN YOUR VISIT

ADDRESS : 71 N 2nd Avenue, Dodge City, KS 67801

INFO LINE: (620) 225-8160

WEBSITE: www.dodgecity.org/106/Wright-Park-Zoo

MEMBERSHIP: ks-dodgecity3.civicplus.com/
DocumentCenter/View/9169/FWPZ-Brochure

HOURS

MEMORIAL DAY–LABOR DAY: Mon–Sat: 9:00 am–5:00 pm
& Sun: 1:00 pm–7:00 pm

LABOR DAY–MEMORIAL DAY: Mon–Sat: 9:00 am–5:00 pm
& Sun: 1:00 pm–5:00 pm

CLOSED: Thanksgiving and Christmas Day

White doves (above) and gray Chinese geese (below) from Wright Park Zoo in Dodge City, KS

ANIMALS

Table of Contents

★ ADDAX ★

Addax nasomaculatus

The addax is a medium-sized spiral-horned antelope. It lives primarily in arid and semi-arid regions of North Africa. It is extinct across most of its former range except for a small population in Niger, though there are efforts underway to introduce them back into their former ranges in Morocco and Tunisia. The addax is well suited to its desert habitat. It can go almost entirely without water, getting it mostly from the plants they eat. Also due to the desert climate, the addax is mainly nocturnal. The primary threat to the addax is poaching for its meat, horns, and hides, followed by oil and gas development in the region in which it lives.

The addax seems to thrive in captivity. While the wild population may only number in the hundreds, the captive population in zoos and breeding facilities around the world is over 600 and on the increase. Whenever I have seen addaxes, they never seem to be in a hurry, which is one thing that would make them vulnerable in the wild. These animals seem quite content to just graze and rest.

CONSERVATION STATUS

CRITICALLY ENDANGERED   ENDANGERED   VULNERABLE   NEAR THREATENED   LEAST CONCERN

Addax from Saint Louis Zoo in Saint Louis, MO

68

Addaxes from Rolling Hills Zoo in Salina, KS (above), and Blank Park Zoo in Des Moines, IA (below)

AFRICAN BUSH ELEPHANT

Loxodonta africana

The African elephant is the world's largest terrestrial animal. Typically, the African elephants found in zoos are the Bush species and not the Forest species, which is closely related but smaller. Elephants are social mammals, with herds consisting of females and juveniles led by a matriarch. They are widespread over most of Eastern and Southern Africa. The biggest threat to elephants is habitat loss and fragmentation due to growing human populations and poaching for their ivory. Despite worldwide bans on ivory trading, the number of elephants killed each year is significant.

Elephants are one of the animals I really enjoy watching at the zoo. They are extremely intelligent and are generally considered to be as smart as primates, dolphins, or whales. They seem to spend their time interacting, communicating, and playing with each other. One of my favorite places to observe elephants is at Sedgwick County Zoo where a small herd of six individuals was brought after being rescued from a drought in Swaziland as part of an ongoing effort to provide them with a safe environment. They are truly magnificent creatures, and I always look forward to seeing them.

CONSERVATION STATUS

CRITICALLY ENDANGERED	ENDANGERED	VULNERABLE	NEAR THREATENED	LEAST CONCERN

African bush elephant from Sedgwick County Zoo in Wichita, KS

African bush elephants from Kansas City Zoo in Kansas City, MO (above), and Henry Doorly Zoo in Omaha, NE (below)

★ AFRICAN PENGUIN ★

Spheniscus demersus

🐾 The only species of penguin to nest in Africa, the African penguin is easily recognizable by the pink patch above each eye. Their range is along the ocean shores of Southeastern Africa, principally in Namibia and South Africa. African penguins primarily feed on anchovies, herrings, and sardines, which has put them under severe threat due to overfishing by offshore fishing operations. This penguin species belongs to the family of banded penguins, so-called because of the black band that runs around their bodies. This family is also known for their loud vocalizations. The African penguin and other members of this penguin family are some of the northernmost penguins, but they still rely on cold ocean currents for their survival.

🔭 Penguins are one of my favorite animals to see at a zoo. With their tuxedo coats, they look like they are ready for a black-tie event. They are also a very friendly sort and will often come right up to the edge of the enclosure to say hello. African penguins are one of the more common penguin species to see at a zoo as they do not generally require a cold room to thrive. The other common species are Humboldt and Magellanic penguins, both of which are also members of the same banded penguin family. However, the real beauty of watching penguins is in seeing them in the water. They are masters of the element, nimble and quick. It is easy to see how they can catch fast, small fish for dinner.

CONSERVATION STATUS

| CRITICALLY ENDANGERED | **ENDANGERED** | VULNERABLE | NEAR THREATENED | LEAST CONCERN |

African penguin from Roosevelt Park Zoo in Minot, ND

African penguins from Tanganyika Wildlife Park in Goddard, KS (above), and Minnesota Zoo in Apple Valley, MN (below)

★ AFRICAN WILD DOG ★

Lycaon pictus

The largest of the African canids, the African wild dog does not actually belong to the genus *Canis*, which includes wolves, coyotes, jackals, and domestic dogs. Rather, they are the only living members of their own family called *Lycaon*. The African wild dog is a highly social animal and can form large packs at times. They are similar to lions in their versatility and adaptability, inhabiting a range of environments. Their former range was nearly all sub-Saharan Africa, but today they are isolated to a few remaining pockets of territory, mostly in the southern part of the African continent. A rare quality among pack animals, it is the females who leave the pack when they come of age. They set off to find a new pack, while young males remain with the group.

African wild dogs always seem very curious about the world and what is going on around them. They seemingly always have something new to investigate. They appear to have three modes: sleep, observe, and patrol. I enjoy seeing the coats of random markings they sport. Each one appears to be unique, and scientists speculate this helps them identify one another in the wild.

CONSERVATION STATUS

| CRITICALLY ENDANGERED | ENDANGERED | VULNERABLE | NEAR THREATENED | LEAST CONCERN |

African wild dog from Rolling Hills Zoo in Salina, KS

African wild dogs from Sedgwick County Zoo in Wichita, KS (above), and Great Plains Zoo in Sioux Falls, SD (below)

★ ALDABRA GIANT TORTOISE ★

Aldabrachelys gigantea

The Aldabra giant tortoise is thought to be the last extant giant tortoise in the Indian Ocean. There were several species spread across that ocean, but most were hunted to extinction for their meat in the 19th century. This tortoise lives predominantly on Aldabra Atoll, which is the second-largest coral atoll in the world and part of the Seychelles group of islands. It is a voracious grazer and plays a similar role on the island as the elephant does in Africa by felling trees and creating trails across the island for other animals to use as they travel. Like most giant tortoise species, Aldabra giant tortoises are long-lived with lifespans over 150 years and even longer in captivity. They were also one of the very first animals to have a direct conservation effort made on their behalf, going all the way back to the end of the 19th century.

These big tortoises always fascinate me. They remind me of a bulldozer leveling everything in its path as they graze on vegetation, leaving it the height of a well-kept putting green. Due to their grazing style, in the wild plants have adapted to form what is called "tortoise turf," which is comprised of a mix of over 20 herbs and grasses, most of which seed near the ground instead of near their top. These tortoises are very adaptable to captivity and will outlive generations of keepers. Currently, Esmeralda is the longest living Aldabra giant tortoise. Living in the Seychelles, he is also the largest, weighing in at about 800 pounds.

CONSERVATION STATUS

CRITICALLY ENDANGERED	ENDANGERED	VULNERABLE	NEAR THREATENED	LEAST CONCERN

Aldabra giant tortoise from Blank Park Zoo in Des Moines, IA

Aldabra giant tortoises from Saint Louis Zoo in Saint Louis, MO (above), and Rolling Hills Zoo in Salina, KS (below)

AMERICAN ALLIGATOR

Alligator mississippiensis

The American alligator is something of a conservation success story. By the 1960s, it was listed as endangered, but proper management and protection have brought it back. They are an important keystone species in their environments, not only because they are a top predator but also because of how they transform their environment through the creation of alligator holes. These holes play a critical role in increasing the diversity of plants and animals in wetland areas by creating small ponds. Large alligators keep the environment healthy by feeding on indigenous animals like muskrat and introduced animals like the coypu, both of which can severely damage wetlands with their burrows. Unlike their cousins the crocodiles, both the American and Chinese species of alligator can live in colder climates, so at times they may be found far north of their traditional ranges. The American alligator is endemic to most of the Southeastern United States, from Virginia in the east to Texas in the west and as far north as parts of Oklahoma and Arkansas.

There is something primeval about watching a sizable alligator at the zoo. While the American alligator has only existed for about 20 million years, crocodilians as a group have been around for over 100 million years. In a real sense, watching an alligator is like staring far back into the history of life on this planet. Because of their adaptability, they often do well in captivity. One of my favorite alligator exhibits is at the Saint Louis Zoo, but because it has a lot of vegetation, it is better for viewing than for taking pictures.

CONSERVATION STATUS

CRITICALLY ENDANGERED   ENDANGERED   VULNERABLE   NEAR THREATENED   **LEAST CONCERN**

American alligator from Bramble Park Zoo in Watertown, SD

American alligators from Dakota Zoo in Bismarck, ND (above), and Chahinkapa Zoo in Wahpeton, ND (below)

★ AMERICAN PLAINS BISON ★

Bison bison bison

The American Plains bison is the largest herbivore in North America. A mature male bison can measure up to six feet tall and weigh over a ton. In the 1700s, there were an estimated 40 million bison roaming all the way from Virginia in the southeast to Alaska in the northwest. However, by 1890 this number had dropped to just over 500 due to slaughter and diseases from domestic cattle. The species was saved from extinction by the concerted effort of ranchers and conservationists. The bison was a vital keystone species of the Great Plains, modifying the environment to allow for a greater diversity of plants and animals. Likewise, the bison played a critical role in maintaining the shortgrass prairies of the Great Plains.

The American Plains bison is one of my favorite animals. I have photographed them not only in zoos but at several conservation sites across the Midwest. They are magnificent creatures who seem to go unhurriedly through their day. They move slowly from spot to spot, periodically stopping to graze when they have space to roam. However, bison are very dangerous animals. When they feel threatened, they can charge at nearly 40 miles per hour, so they must be given a lot of space. Bison are responsible for more injuries in national parks than bears.

CONSERVATION STATUS

CRITICALLY ENDANGERED   ENDANGERED   VULNERABLE   **NEAR THREATENED**   LEAST CONCERN

American Plains bison from Great Plains Zoo in Sioux Falls, SD

American Plains bison from Bramble Park Zoo in Watertown, SD (above), and
Minnesota Zoo in Apple Valley, MN (below)

American Plains bison from Lee G. Simmons Wildlife Safari Park in Ashland, NE (above), and Como Park Zoo in Saint Paul, MN (below)

American Plains bison from Riverside Discovery Center in Scottsbluff, NE (above), and Sedgwick County Zoo in Wichita, KS (below)

AMERICAN BLACK BEAR

Ursus americanus

🐾 **The smallest bear in North America, the** American black bear was once widespread across the entire continent. Nowadays, other than in Arkansas, Louisiana, and the northern Great Lakes region, it can no longer be found between the Appalachian Mountains and the Rocky Mountains. Though it is called the black bear, it can range in color from black to brown to cinnamon, sometimes even in the same litter of cubs. The color seems to be geographically related, with darker bears in the east and lighter colored bears in the west. There is even a subspecies in Canada that has a high percentage of bears with white fur. The American black bear is omnivorous, but most of its diet is plants and insects, which is similar to its larger cousin the brown bear.

🔭 **I like watching bears, particularly black** bears. As with so many of the animals I seem to favor, they are very smart and very inquisitive about what is happening around them. Though sometimes that inquisitiveness can get them in a spot of trouble, like the bear in the Topeka Zoo pictured on the next pages. He was able to climb up the tree easily enough, but getting down was more of a challenge. Despite this, black bears are one of the largest arboreal species in North America. They are also very adaptable and have been able to survive even near urban spaces, often bringing them into conflict with humans. Unfortunately, bears are often the losers in these conflicts, because they become more aggressive when acclimated to people.

CONSERVATION STATUS

CRITICALLY ENDANGERED	ENDANGERED	VULNERABLE	NEAR THREATENED	LEAST CONCERN

American black bear from Great Plains Zoo in Sioux Falls, SD

American black bears from Minnesota Zoo in Apple Valley, MN (above), and Lee G. Simmons Wildlife Safari Park in Ashland, NE (below)

American black bears from Topeka Zoo in Topeka, KS (above), and
Minnesota Zoo in Apple Valley, MN (below)

American black bears from Dickerson Park Zoo in Springfield, MO (above), and Great Plains Zoo in Sioux Falls, SD (below)

★ AMUR TIGER ★

Panthera tigris altaica

Once thought to be a separate species from other tigers, it is now known through DNA analysis that the Amur, or Siberian, tiger is just one of several subspecies. It is the largest subspecies of extant tiger, being slightly larger than the Bengal tiger. A male can be six and a half feet long without the tail and weigh over 500 pounds. It is believed the Amur tiger and extinct Caspian tiger migrated north from eastern China along what would later become the Silk Road. The two subspecies form the northern group of tigers, and the remaining Asian tigers form the southern group. They are strict carnivores and an apex predator in their range. The Amur tiger was once widespread along the northeastern part of Asia from Siberia to China, but now it is only in isolated pockets mostly in Russia along the Sikhote-Alin mountain range and may number less than 600 in the wild.

It is well known that most cats do not like water, but tigers are hot tubbing fools who love being in the water. You can often find them in zoos lounging in the pools provided for them. Like most large carnivores, the Amur tiger spends most of its time resting to conserve energy, so it sometimes takes several visits to their enclosures to get a good picture of them being active. But patience is often rewarded because when they are active, they are very playful and often splash in the water. These tigers are in one of the most successful and longest-running Species Survival Plans, with now over 160 individuals under its purview. The program has become a model for running other programs to save endangered species. And, tiger conservation efforts in the wild benefit other large animals like the Asian black bear and Roe deer.

CONSERVATION STATUS

| CRITICALLY ENDANGERED | **ENDANGERED** | VULNERABLE | NEAR THREATENED | LEAST CONCERN |

Amur tiger from Sedgwick County Zoo in Wichita, KS

Amur tigers from Bramble Park Zoo in Watertown, SD (above), and
Minnesota Zoo in Apple Valley, MN (below)

Amur tigers from Rolling Hills Zoo in Salina, KS (above), and
Riverside Discovery Center in Scottsbluff, NE (below)

Amur tigers from Henry Doorly Zoo in Omaha, NE (above), and
Saint Louis Zoo in Saint Louis, MO (below)

★ ARCTIC FOX ★

Vulpes lagopus

The Arctic fox is a small, round, and compact member of the fox family. In many areas its primary food source is lemmings, and so it follows that the fox population rises and falls as the population of lemmings fluctuates. The Arctic fox also preys on many other small animals and has a taste for berries as well. The winter coat of most Arctic foxes is bright white, providing excellent camouflage in the snow. The fur then turns brownish gray in the summer. While the species overall is not threatened, individual populations like the one in Sweden and Norway were hunted to near extinction. Arctic foxes are good long-distance travelers and will sometimes cover hundreds of miles in their journeys through their Arctic home.

Arctic foxes seem only to have two speeds, on or off. They spend their days either sleeping or playing at full speed. During one trip to Great Plains Zoo, two Arctic foxes were having great fun chasing each other around the enclosure in what could only be described as a game of tag. One would playfully nip the other and take off at full speed for the other end, while the now "it" fox would give spirited chase.

CONSERVATION STATUS

| CRITICALLY ENDANGERED | ENDANGERED | VULNERABLE | NEAR THREATENED | LEAST CONCERN |

Arctic fox from Great Plains Zoo in Sioux Falls, SD

Arctic foxes from Dakota Zoo in Bismarck, ND (above), and Como Park Zoo in Saint Paul, MN (below)

BACTRIAN CAMEL (WILD)

Camelus ferus

🐾 The name Bactrian camel can refer to one of two species of camel. It was believed until recently that wild camels were simply feral camels from the domesticated species. However, recent evidence suggests the species split from one another over a million years ago. The wild species can be distinguished by the narrower and more conical shaped humps on their back. While the wild Bactrian camel once ranged over much of Northwest China and most of Mongolia, it is now isolated to a few disconnected areas. These wild camels are under serious threat mostly from poaching for their meat and from human activity such as mining and agriculture. There are now only about 1400 left in the wild, and they are considered the eighth most endangered species in the world.

🔭 The camel, in general, is a pretty ugly creature, but in that ugliness lies their beauty and their charm, at least for me. I enjoy watching camels at the zoo as they eat their food or just stroll around the enclosure in their ungainly gait. They are just plain fun to watch and rather always remind me of old men. I never thought much about camels as swimmers until I saw a camel family at the Minnesota Zoo all hanging out in the water as if it was a perfectly natural place for them to be. It was a hot day after all.

CONSERVATION STATUS

CRITICALLY ENDANGERED   ENDANGERED   VULNERABLE   NEAR THREATENED   LEAST CONCERN

Wild Bactrian camels from Minnesota Zoo in Apple Valley, MN

Wild Bactrian camels from Great Plains Zoo in Sioux Falls, SD (above), and Red River Zoo in Fargo, ND (below)

★ BIGHORN SHEEP ★

Ovis canadensis

The bighorn sheep can be found in the Rocky Mountains and Sierra Nevadas from the Baja California Peninsula in Mexico to southwestern Canada. There is also a distinct subspecies that lives in the deserts of the Southwest United States. The Rocky Mountain subspecies can grow quite large, standing up to three and a half feet at the shoulders and weighing more than 500 pounds. Bighorn sheep are herbivores that feed mainly on grasses in the summer and shrubs in the winter. Being closely related to domestic sheep, they are very susceptible to the diseases from these flocks. Typically, an outbreak will cause a near complete die-off of the infected population and long-term effects that slow recovery.

The bighorn sheep is right up there with the American bison as one of the most majestic species in North America. With their giant horns and large size, they cut a very noble image. One of the reasons I like to see them at the zoo, especially in the late spring and early summer, is because they produce adorable babies. When young, the babies are spindly and clumsy, but within a year they grow into their adult form. Another fun thing about seeing bighorn sheep is their tendency to find a seat upon the very highest spot, just like the big fellow below from Hemker Park and Zoo who decided to rest atop the feeder filled with hay.

CONSERVATION STATUS

CRITICALLY ENDANGERED   ENDANGERED   VULNERABLE   NEAR THREATENED   **LEAST CONCERN**

Bighorn sheep from Hemker Park and Zoo in Freeport, MN

Bighorn sheep from Dakota Zoo in Bismarck, ND (above), and Great Plains Zoo in Sioux Falls, SD (below)

★ BLACK-AND-WHITE COLOBUS ★

Colobus angolensis

The type of black-and-white colobus typically found in zoos is the Angolan colobus. They live across the southern part of Africa in the Democratic Republic of the Congo and eastern Tanzania. Although named after the country of Angola, they are relatively rare there aside from a narrow strip along the northeastern border. Angolan colobuses are old world monkeys, meaning monkeys from Africa or Asia, that generally lack a prehensile tail like new world monkeys. There are six different subspecies of the Angolan colobus, which are defined mainly by the geographical region and environment they inhabit. They are a very adaptable species and can tolerate a broad range of temperatures, from tropical forests to altitudes of a mile and half high on mountains.

The black-and-white colobus is a regular sight at zoos. One likely reason for this is their very adaptable nature that allows them to survive in many different environments. Overall, there are five species of black-and-white colobus, but it can be tough to tell them apart when seeing them at the zoo. Another common species found in zoos is the mantled guereza, also called the eastern black-and-white colobus. Usually, black-and-white colobus monkeys can be seen relaxing in their family group and when not resting, can sometimes engage in vigorous play. This is when they are the most fun to photograph but also the most challenging because of their constant movement.

CONSERVATION STATUS

| CRITICALLY ENDANGERED | ENDANGERED | VULNERABLE | NEAR THREATENED | **LEAST CONCERN** |

Black-and-white colobuses from Tanganyika Wildlife Park in Goddard, KS

Black-and-white colobuses from Henry Doorly Zoo in Omaha, NE (above), and Lincoln Children's Zoo in Lincoln, NE (below)

★ BLACK SWAN ★

Cygnus atratus

Black swans are a sizeable aquatic bird from Australia. Like most swans, the black swan is an herbivore that feeds primarily on aquatic plants, though it will come ashore and feed on grasses and other plants when their typical food is scarce. This swan is rare among animals in that it pairs for life. In swans, however, this pair-bonding behavior is typical. It is a beautiful bird and has been introduced all over the world in gardens and ornamental water features. In its home range, it can be very nomadic depending on rainfall amounts. It has been known to travel hundreds of miles to escape drought conditions.

It is still as exciting today to watch a black swan glide through the water with their sleek black plumage, as I am sure it was a hundred years ago. They are a common animal to find in zoos today because, like other common animals, they are highly adaptable. There are now wild colonies of black swans all over the world, from England to China to Japan. In New Zealand, there are colonies of black swans that were both introduced and that arrived on their own, showing their ability to survive and prosper in a variety of climatic conditions.

CONSERVATION STATUS

CRITICALLY ENDANGERED   ENDANGERED   VULNERABLE   NEAR THREATENED   **LEAST CONCERN**

Black swans from Blank Park Zoo in Des Moines, IA

Black swans from Great Plains Zoo in Sioux Falls, SD (above), and Sedgwick County Zoo in Wichita, KS (below)

BLACK-TAILED PRAIRIE DOG

Cynomys ludovicianus

The black-tailed prairie dog was once as ubiquitous on the western Great Plains as the bison. Their territory range covered Arizona in the south and followed north along the eastern side of the Rocky Mountains into Canada. The prairie dog is considered a keystone species, especially in shortgrass prairies where their tunnels enrich the soil and their voracious appetites keep the grasses and other plants in check. Their populations have been significantly reduced over the years, by up to 98 percent in some cases, but they are still numerous in most parts of the Plains. Predominantly herbivores, they will supplement their diet with the occasional grasshopper or two. The prairie dog lives in large "towns," which may have hundreds of burrows. These prairie dog towns are important for other wildlife, as burrowing owls and black-footed ferrets will occupy unused burrows.

Prairie dogs are just downright fun to watch. They will scamper around eating, playing, and standing guard in turn. They are social animals and seem to spend a fair amount of time grooming and cuddling each other. They are ever watchful though, and as soon as a potential threat is seen, they raise the alarm. Research has shown that prairie dogs have specific calls for different kinds of threats, so the call for a hawk will be different from the one for a coyote. It is believed that not only do they communicate the type of threat but also information about it, like distance and size. And what is a prairie dog to do after a hard morning of prairie dogging? They collapse on the ground right where they are, just like the poor little fellow from David Traylor Zoo pictured below, who was just plain tuckered out.

CONSERVATION STATUS

| CRITICALLY ENDANGERED | ENDANGERED | VULNERABLE | NEAR THREATENED | LEAST CONCERN |

Black-tailed prairie dog from David Traylor Zoo in Emporia, KS

Black-tailed prairie dogs from Sunset Zoo in Manhattan, KS (above), and Minnesota Zoo in Apple Valley, MN (below)

Black-tailed prairie dogs from Hutchinson Zoo in Hutchinson, KS (above), and Red River Zoo in Fargo, ND (below)

Black-tailed prairie dogs from Bramble Park Zoo in Watertown, SD (above), and Dakota Zoo in Bismarck, ND (below)

★ BOBCAT ★

Lynx rufus

🐾 The bobcat is the smallest of the Lynx family, though large males may be bigger than its close relative, the Canadian lynx. They look much like a large domestic cat and exhibit some very cat-like behavior. This medium-sized cat may be found across the United States and as far north as southern Canada and as far south as Central Mexico. The bobcat is highly adaptable, inhabiting a variety of environments from swamps to mountains. As long as there is sufficient prey, dense cover, and nooks and crannies for hiding, there will probably be a bobcat lurking around. The only terrain really not suited to them is open cropland. Their primary prey are rabbits and rodents, but they can switch preferred species as the seasons change or as different prey become available.

🔭 The bobcat is an exception in that they are not very adaptable to living in zoos. In fact, for all their abundance in the wild, they are a rare find in zoos, so it is always a treat to find one. It is easy to tell that bobcats are in the same big family as domestic cats, Felinae. In fact, for a long time, they were thought to belong to the same genus as domestic cats, *Felis*. They spend their days mostly sleeping, with occasional breaks to groom themselves or stalk whatever unfortunate mouse happened to come across their enclosure. I watched the one in Dakota Zoo, pictured opposite, stalk something for about 10 minutes before it finally decided a nap sounded much better. I am not sure what it thought it saw or if there was even something there to begin with, but it was fun to watch.

CONSERVATION STATUS

CRITICALLY ENDANGERED	ENDANGERED	VULNERABLE	NEAR THREATENED	LEAST CONCERN

Bobcats from Hutchinson Zoo in Hutchinson, KS

Bobcats from Dakota Zoo in Bismarck, ND (above), and Lincoln Children's Zoo in Lincoln, NE (below)

CALIFORNIA SEA LION

Zalophus californianus

The California sea lion is a pinniped, the clade representing seals, sea lions, and walruses, and is native to the western coastline of North America. Its home range and breeding grounds stretch from central California to the Gulf of California on the eastern side of the Baja California Peninsula. However, males often journey even farther from there, reaching as far as Alaska in one direction and Panama in the other direction. California sea lions are excellent hunters, eating a wide variety of fish and squid. They are also comfortable for short stretches in freshwater and may travel a hundred miles or more inland in search of a tasty fish dinner. They are remarkably intelligent and have a wide range of vocalizations. While the California sea lion is a predator, it is also prey for sharks and mammal-eating killer whales.

Most people think the lion is one of the loudest animals in the zoo, but a big male California sea lion will give any lion a run for its money. They are not just loud for a moment like a lion, but are continuously loud for up to an hour or more and can often be heard everywhere in the zoo. They are inquisitive and highly intelligent, particularly when interacting with their keepers or with enrichment items in their enclosures. The California sea lion swims with only its front flippers, unlike true seals that use their back flippers. When not swimming the day away, they pull themselves out of the water by turning their back flippers inward and walking on all fours until they find a warm, sunny spot for a snooze.

CONSERVATION STATUS

CRITICALLY ENDANGERED   ENDANGERED   VULNERABLE   NEAR THREATENED   **LEAST CONCERN**

California sea lions from Henry Doorly Zoo in Omaha, NE

California sea lions from Saint Louis Zoo in Saint Louis, MO (above), and
Blank Park Zoo in Des Moines, IA (below)

★ CARIBOU ★

Rangifer tarandus

👣 **The caribou, or reindeer, is a large species of** deer living in northern North America and Eurasia. The caribou is divided roughly into two groups based on whether they are migratory or not. One subspecies, the Porcupine caribou, migrates over 1500 miles from northern Alaska and the Yukon Territory to inland boreal forests. It is one of the longest migrations of any land animal. It is the only species of deer that is semi-domesticated. In Siberia and Scandinavia, caribou have been herded by people for at least 3000 years. They are kept for their milk, meat, and transportation, but those traditions are gradually being lost in modern times. In North America, they do not have the same history of domestication, but even so, the vast herds were crucial to the native peoples of Canada.

🔭 **There is something about the massive racks** of antlers on caribou that makes them very fun to see in a zoo. It is the only species of deer in which both the males and females have antlers. In older males, the antlers can grow to be quite large, in some cases over three feet across with a length of over four feet. The old fellow from the Minnesota Zoo pictured below is pretty close to those measurements. Another interesting fact about the antlers is that females lose theirs in the late spring or early summer right before calving. In the warmer months of summer, caribou can often be found resting in their enclosures, usually in a nicely shaded spot. But like their wild brethren, they are also fond of moving around and often leave well-worn trails for others to follow.

CONSERVATION STATUS

CRITICALLY ENDANGERED   ENDANGERED   VULNERABLE   NEAR THREATENED   LEAST CONCERN

Caribou from Minnesota Zoo in Apple Valley, MN

Caribou from Hemker Park and Zoo in Freeport, MN (above), and Como Park Zoo in Saint Paul, MN (below)

CHEETAH

Acinonyx jubatus

The cheetah is one of only two species of cats to have been domesticated. It is a large cat that once lived from Southern Africa through the Middle East and over to India. Now it is concentrated in Southern and Eastern Africa with a small group in northeastern Iran. The cheetah is swift and can reach a top speed of nearly 70 miles per hour over a short distance. It hunts its prey, usually antelopes, by stalking closely and then attacking at high speed. Unlike other cats, it cannot retract its claws, so they are generally dull but useful for high-speed maneuvering. In overall build, they resemble dogs more than cats. The cheetah is under pressure from several human activities, particularly agriculture, game farms, and roads. The last is thought to account for a significant number of cheetah deaths each year, especially where the roads cross through wildlife preserves and national parks.

The cheetah has been one of my favorite animals since early childhood. I was always impressed by their speed and their overall seemingly friendly disposition. They are well known for their lack of fear of humans. While in ancient times this made them easy to tame, in modern times it has led to conflict between these big cats and humans. I enjoy stopping for a long time when I come to the cheetah enclosures, especially if they are active. When they take off at a dead sprint, it is a sight to behold. I have only been able to capture that once, but because the cat was moving so fast, the picture turned out a bit blurry. I hope I get more chances for a photograph like that in my future travels. The picture below from the Saint Louis Zoo was taken just a second before the animal took off at full speed. It was so fast, my poor camera could not capture a good picture.

CONSERVATION STATUS

CRITICALLY ENDANGERED	ENDANGERED	VULNERABLE	NEAR THREATENED	LEAST CONCERN

Cheetah from Saint Louis Zoo in Saint Louis, MO

Cheetahs from Dickerson Park Zoo in Springfield, MO (above), and Henry Doorly Zoo in Omaha, NE (below)

★ CHILEAN FLAMINGO ★

Phoenicopterus chilensis

The Chilean flamingo can be found geographically in a narrow strip running from Ecuador down through Peru, Bolivia, Chile, and finally, most of Argentina. While they are called Chilean flamingos, only a small portion of their range is actually in Chile. In fact, the most significant part covers most of Argentina. Like all flamingos, the Chilean flamingo is a filter feeder that strains plankton and small invertebrates from the shallow lakes they inhabit. They are a very hardy species and can be found at elevations as high as two and a half miles. Chilean flamingos gather in large flocks in brackish or alkaline lakes, often with the other two South American flamingo species, the Andean flamingo and Puna flamingo. Their bright pink color is not just from eating brine shrimp but also comes from the other things that compose their diet. As with the other flamingos of South America, they are under threat from human activity, specifically from mining, egg collecting, and the irrigation of farmland.

There is nothing quite like the sight of a flock of flamingos all standing together each on one leg. This flamingo species is a relatively common one in zoos due to its hardiness. Chilean flamingos are quite striking birds with their black beaks and black flight feathers. Like all flamingos, they are quite vocal and often noisy. They have a honking type of call, which is very similar to a goose but deeper in pitch. It is easy to tell this species apart because of their black-and-white bill, black flight feathers, and bright red knees. Chilean flamingos do very well in captivity, often living 40 years or more.

CONSERVATION STATUS

CRITICALLY ENDANGERED   ENDANGERED   VULNERABLE   **NEAR THREATENED**   LEAST CONCERN

Chilean flamingos from Lee Richardson Zoo in Garden City, KS

Chilean flamingos from Blank Park Zoo in Des Moines, IA (above), and Como Park Zoo in Saint Paul, MN (below)

CHImPANZEE

Pan troglodytes

Chimpanzees and their cousins the bonobos are the closest living relatives to humans. It is estimated we share as much as 98 percent of our DNA. Chimpanzees live in the forest belt of Africa from Cameroon to Tanzania north of the Congo River and along the western coast of Africa from Senegal to Ivory Coast. While predominantly a forest species, they are quite adaptable, occupying terrains like savannas and open woodlands as well. Chimpanzees mainly eat fruits but supplement their diet with a variety of other things, including meat they hunt. They are highly intelligent animals and have learned to use tools to solve a variety of problems they face in the wild. The chimpanzee is a protected species in most of its range, but that has not stopped threats like deforestation, mining, poaching, and human diseases from taking their toll on them. Their population has been severely reduced in most areas, and the outlook is for further decline over the next decade.

Chimpanzees are not often seen in zoos. They require very specialized care and a lot of daily enrichment to thrive and be happy. When they are in a zoo, I am always curious to watch them and see what culture they have learned from their environment. In the wild, these cultural traditions are passed down within groups and can be very specialized in different regions. I often wonder as I stand there watching them if they are also watching us humans, trying to figure out the monkeys on the other side of the glass. One particularly good chimpanzee enclosure is in the Kansas City Zoo. They have an entire forested hillside to explore, and come dinner time, they all come scrambling down the hill to get to the food like you can see in the picture below.

CONSERVATION STATUS

CRITICALLY ENDANGERED | **ENDANGERED** | VULNERABLE | NEAR THREATENED | LEAST CONCERN

Chimpanzees from Kansas City Zoo in Kansas City, MO

Chimpanzees from Sedgwick County Zoo in Wichita, KS (above), and
Saint Louis Zoo in Saint Louis, MO (below)

★ COTTON-TOP TAMARIN ★

Saguinus oedipus

🐾 The cotton-top tamarin is one of the rarest primates in the world, with only about 6000 left in the wild. In the wild, they live in small family groups, which can have as many as 9 to 13 members. These little primates are omnivores, with fruit and insects comprising most of their diet. Cotton-top tamarins, like other members of their family, are unique in that, unlike most primates, they regularly give birth to twins. Parental duties are handled by all the adult members of the group, but especially by the father. Cotton-top tamarin society places a great emphasis on cooperation and altruism. They are also highly intelligent with a well-developed communication system that has elements of grammar. Young tamarins may understand some of it but must learn how to communicate as they get older.

🔭 These little guys are a bundle of energy, which makes them fun to watch but sometimes hard to photograph. Cotton-top tamarins are very inquisitive, and many times they will get as close as they can to me to see what I am doing. I think they are some of the best natural hams for the camera. The little fellow and his buddies from Rolling Hills Zoo certainly were. You can see him posing for his picture below. These tamarins were certainly very interested in what I was doing and kept coming right up to the edge of the enclosure to take a closer look. When I finally turned to leave, they started chattering loudly as if to say, "wait, we are not finished with you yet!" It made me laugh for the rest of the day thinking about the cotton-top hams.

CONSERVATION STATUS

CRITICALLY ENDANGERED ENDANGERED VULNERABLE NEAR THREATENED LEAST CONCERN

Cotton-top tamarin from Rolling Hills Zoo in Salina, KS

Cotton-top tamarins from Lincoln Children's Zoo in Lincoln, NE (above), and Saint Louis Zoo in Saint Louis, MO (below)

COUGAR

Puma concolor

The cougar is a large cat native to North and South America. It can be found from the Yukon in the north to Patagonia in the south. This big cat is adaptable and lives in a wide variety of environments. Because of this, it is also a generalist when it comes to its prey. In Argentina, the cougar's favorite food is the guanaco, while in the temperate forests of South Dakota, it feeds primarily on white-tailed deer. Because of this large variety of prey, it is the most widespread large mammal in the Western Hemisphere. The cougar is mostly a solitary animal and defends a significant territory whose size depends on the abundance of prey. Conflict with humans was relatively rare in the past but has significantly increased as humans have taken over more and more places where it lives.

When watching a cougar at the zoo, it is interesting to see how much like domestic cats they are. One possible reason for this is that they are from the same subfamily as house cats and are not related to lions, tigers, or jaguars. However, they do share one thing in common with other big cats: a love of naps. They will spend large parts of their day napping or resting, often preceded by a great big yawn, as demonstrated by the cougar in the picture below from Rolling Hills Zoo. When they are not getting some shut-eye, cougars actively like to explore their enclosures, looking for food or unusual smells. Like the American black bear, they are also moving into urban areas and become very adept at thriving in these new environments.

CONSERVATION STATUS

CRITICALLY ENDANGERED	ENDANGERED	VULNERABLE	NEAR THREATENED	LEAST CONCERN

Cougar from Rolling Hills Zoo in Salina, KS

Cougars from Topeka Zoo in Topeka, KS (above), and Minnesota Zoo in Apple Valley, MN (below)

EASTERN BLACK RHINOCEROS

Diceros bicornis michaeli

There are five species of rhinoceros, and they are all endangered. They are one of the most endangered species in the world. The eastern black rhinoceros pictured in these pages is down to just over 500 individuals in the wild. These large herbivores once ranged over much of Africa but are now limited to a few pockets in Kenya and Tanzania. There are five subspecies of black rhinoceros recognized by the International Union for Conservation of Nature (IUCN), of which two are extinct. The majority of black rhinos in zoos are the eastern subspecies because it is so critically endangered in the wild. The biggest threat to both species of rhinoceros, white and black, in Africa is illegal poaching for their horns, which has caused their numbers to drop by more than 90 percent in some cases.

There is something prehistoric about seeing a rhinoceros at the zoo. Rhinoceroses are big, armored, and full of attitude. These creatures are also a wonderful sight to behold with their horns and ears that rotate around. I like taking pictures of them because each one has a different personality, and some really seem to enjoy posing for the camera. Rhinos are surprisingly fast for their size and can reach speeds of 30 miles per hour on open ground. The black rhinoceros is a bit smaller than its cousin the white rhinoceros. It is easy to tell the two species apart, even though they are similarly gray in color, when you see them in the zoo just by looking at their mouths. If it is flat and broad, it is a white rhinoceros, and if it is pointed, it is a black rhinoceros. This is because the white rhino is a grazer that feeds mostly on grass, and the black rhino is a browser that feeds on leaves and branches.

CONSERVATION STATUS

CRITICALLY ENDANGERED   ENDANGERED   VULNERABLE   NEAR THREATENED   LEAST CONCERN

Eastern black rhinoceros from Saint Louis Zoo in Saint Louis, MO

Eastern black rhinoceroses from Great Plains Zoo in Sioux Falls, SD (above), and
Kansas City Zoo in Kansas City, MO (below)

Eastern black rhinoceroses from Sedgwick County Zoo in Wichita, KS (above), and Blank Park Zoo in Des Moines, IA (below)

Eastern black rhinoceroses from Kansas City Zoo in Kansas City, MO (above), and Great Plains Zoo in Sioux Falls, SD (below)

★ EMU ★

Dromaius novaehollandiae

The emu is a large flightless bird native to Australia. Only the ostrich is taller than the emu. The emu can reach a height of over five feet. It is an omnivore that feeds mainly on plants and seeds. They can also travel long distances to find new sources of food and freshwater. The emu is a fast runner and can achieve speeds of 30 miles per hour. These animals are also known to exhibit different behaviors based on where they are from in Australia. In the western parts of the continent, they seem to follow a seasonal migration pattern, while in the eastern region, there is no clear pattern. The emu is rare among species in that the female is the one who courts the male and may become very aggressive during the breeding season, whereas the male is the one who tends the eggs and raises the hatchlings.

Like the rhino, there is something vaguely prehistoric about the emu. They are fascinating to watch but are rarely excited to see my camera. Typically, if the emus notice me with my camera, they bob their heads and strut around their enclosure. In some ways, this movement makes them very hard to photograph. On the other hand, when they have no interest in me, they go about their business of pecking at the ground and eating whatever they find. In this regard, the emu reminds me of an extra large barnyard chicken. These days that is not far from the truth. Along with ostriches, emus are raised commercially for their meat, eggs, oil, and feathers. Emu ranching has become a boutique farming practice in many places throughout the world.

CONSERVATION STATUS

CRITICALLY ENDANGERED	ENDANGERED	VULNERABLE	NEAR THREATENED	LEAST CONCERN

Emu from Great Plains Zoo in Sioux Falls, SD

Emus from Bramble Park Zoo in Watertown, SD (above), and Sedgwick County Zoo in Wichita, KS (below)

★ GIANT ANTEATER ★

Myrmecophaga tridactyla

The giant anteater is easily recognizable by its long narrow snout and bushy tail. They also have formidable claws on their front legs, which can even deter a jaguar. They use their front claws to dig into insect nests, and then they use their long tongue like a machine gun to slurp up the insects from inside the nest. Giant anteaters primarily prey upon either ants or termites, depending on their location and the local climate. They are native to Central and South America, ranging from Honduras in the north to northern Argentina in the south. A solitary creature, the giant anteater only socializes with others when it is time to mate, much like the behavior of other members of its extended family, which includes sloths and armadillos.

There is no mistaking a giant anteater when you come across one in the zoo. The long snout and bushy tail are dead giveaways. In warmer weather, they may even switch their sleeping patterns, becoming nocturnal. Very often they can be seen curled up taking a nap during the hottest parts of a summer day. When it is time to rest, the giant anteater will dig a shallow hole in the ground with their front claws, like the one in the picture below from Sunset Zoo. When active, they look rather comical since they walk on their knuckles. But despite appearances, they can move pretty quickly when they want to. In zoos, you will often find them in mixed species enclosures with maned wolves, as the two species seem to get along well.

CONSERVATION STATUS

| CRITICALLY ENDANGERED | ENDANGERED | VULNERABLE | NEAR THREATENED | LEAST CONCERN |

Giant anteater from Sunset Zoo in Manhattan, KS

Giant anteaters from Great Plains Zoo in Sioux Falls, SD (above), and
Sedgwick County Zoo in Wichita, KS (below)

GILA MONSTER

Heloderma suspectum

🐾 The Gila monster is one of two species of poisonous lizards found in North America. The other species is its very close cousin the Mexican beaded lizard. Neither is particularly dangerous to humans; however, a bite from one will cause several days of agonizing pain. Gila monsters are slow-moving lizards, so their diet is primarily composed of eggs and young animals still in the nest. When food is plentiful, they will store fat in their tails, which may make up a significant portion of their body weight. This allows these lizards to survive during times when prey is scarce, when they may eat as little as once every other month. They are excellent climbers and have a fondness for pools of water in the desert when they find them. The Gila monster is under threat from human activity, particularly urban sprawl and habitat destruction.

🔭 Gila monsters are excellent models for photography, as they seem quite content to bask in the warmth of a heat lamp, and when they do move, they do so very slowly. Like their cousins the beaded lizards, their skin is covered in a series of raised bumps, which makes for an interesting composition. When you see them in zoos, they are typically plump creatures, meaning they are well-fed and storing fat. Like all lizards, it is fun to watch Gila monsters move around their enclosure, flicking their tongues to taste and smell their environment. This is what the big guy from Saint Louis Zoo, pictured on the opposite page, was doing the day I saw him. They also seem to be very tolerant of having companions in their enclosure, like the lizard from Hutchinson Zoo also pictured on the opposite page.

CONSERVATION STATUS

CRITICALLY ENDANGERED	ENDANGERED	VULNERABLE	NEAR THREATENED	LEAST CONCERN

Gila monster from Rolling Hills Zoo in Salina, KS

Gila monsters from Hutchinson Zoo in Hutchinson, KS (above), and Saint Louis Zoo in Saint Louis, MO (below)

★ GIRAFFE ★

Giraffa camelopardalis

The giraffe is the tallest living terrestrial animal. There are nine recognized subspecies of giraffe, with the reticulated subspecies being the most common in zoos. It is a large herbivorous browser that feeds mostly on trees and shrubs. Once found throughout most of the savannas of Africa, they are now only found in isolated pockets of their former range. As a whole, the conservation status of giraffes is considered to be vulnerable, with several of the subspecies considered to be critically endangered or endangered, such as the Nubian giraffe, which is the nominate subspecies, meaning it is the subspecies that gives the rest their primary name. The biggest threats to giraffes are deforestation, habitat fragmentation, and territorial pressure from human encroachment.

Giraffes are another of those weird-looking animals that I like to watch in the zoo. They seem so ungainly when they are doing anything other than standing still. Fortunately for picture taking, giraffes are rather sedate and, most of the time, move slowly, making it so much easier to capture a picture of them. Giraffes have a number of interesting features for survival. A giraffe's tongue is dark purple to black and prehensile, allowing them to grasp leaves with it. They have an elongated neck, which does not start growing until after they are born. Even with the long neck, they have the same number of vertebrae—seven—as humans and mice. The horns on their head are living tissue, and on females and juveniles they have tufts of hair on the end. The lovely spotted coat of the giraffe is like a fingerprint, no two are exactly the same and it can be used to tell individual giraffes apart.

CONSERVATION STATUS

CRITICALLY ENDANGERED   ENDANGERED   VULNERABLE   NEAR THREATENED   LEAST CONCERN

Giraffe from Dickerson Park Zoo in Springfield, MO

Giraffes from Blank Park Zoo in Des Moines, IA (above), and Lincoln Children's Zoo in Lincoln, NE (below)

Giraffes from Roosevelt Park Zoo in Minot, ND (above), and Kansas City Zoo in Kansas City, MO (below)

Giraffes from Sedgwick County Zoo in Wichita, KS (above), and Saint Louis Zoo in Saint Louis, MO (below)

GRAY WOLF

Canis lupus

The gray wolf, in its many varieties, was once the most widespread mammal on the planet, ranging from Europe to all but tropical Asia to North America. It has now disappeared from much of that range but is slowly making a comeback. It was once thought that the domestic dog descended from this species, but modern genetic techniques show modern dogs likely descended from a separate species of wolf. The gray wolf is a specialist hunter, but the specific prey it selects to feed on largely depends on availability and geographic location. It is a social animal that lives in packs that range from two to as many as twelve members. These packs are centered around the breeding male and female of the pack, and other members serve in supporting roles for hunting and protection of the pups.

Even in zoos, the gray wolf can be a very elusive creature since a proper enclosure provides many places to hide out, away from the eyes of visitors. However, when they are not being shy and elusive, gray wolves are very active, exploring their enclosure, marking their territory, or just playing with the other members of their pack. The gray wolf from Red River Zoo, pictured opposite, was having quite the romp with its fellow pack mates the day I was there. They were charging all over the enclosure, playing a vigorous game of tag. First, one wolf would chase the others around the space, and then when another got caught, it would be its turn to chase. It was a very fun game to watch, and they were still playing when I came back for a second look.

CONSERVATION STATUS

CRITICALLY ENDANGERED   ENDANGERED   VULNERABLE   NEAR THREATENED   **LEAST CONCERN**

Gray wolf from Lee G. Simmons Wildlife Safari Park in Ashland, NE

Gray wolves from Red River Zoo in Fargo, ND (above), and Minnesota Zoo in Apple Valley, MN (below)

GREVY'S ZEBRA

Equus grevyi

The Grevy's zebra is one of three species of zebra found in Africa. It is the largest wild equine, standing up to five feet tall at the withers. It is also the most endangered of the zebra species, living only in isolated pockets in Kenya and Ethiopia. It once ranged across the horn of Africa from Sudan to Kenya. Like all zebras, the Grevy's zebra is black with white stripes, though this zebra has no stripes on its stomach. It is herbivorous, relying mostly on grasses and legumes for its food. Because of its unique digestive system, it can live on much lower quality food than most other ungulates. The Grevy's zebra faces several threats in the wild, mostly from agriculture, including competition with domestic livestock for food and water and exposure to diseases from domestic livestock. Hunting was once a major threat, but that is no longer the case.

While the zebra might not be on my list of top 10 animals to see at the zoo, I am always happy to get a chance to photograph them, especially one as endangered as the Grevy's zebra. The contrast between their black-and-white stripes and their all-white bellies makes them visually interesting. Whenever I see them, they seem to be content animals, standing around in their group eating a bit of hay or swishing their tails to discourage the flies. One of the better places to see Grevy's zebras in particular is the Saint Louis Zoo, pictured below. The enclosure is set up in such a way to give a very good view of them.

CONSERVATION STATUS

CRITICALLY ENDANGERED	ENDANGERED	VULNERABLE	NEAR THREATENED	LEAST CONCERN

Grevy's zebras from Saint Louis Zoo in Saint Louis, MO

Grevy's zebras from Tanganyika Wildlife Park in Goddard, KS (above), and
Great Plains Zoo in Sioux Falls, SD (below)

GRIZZLY BEAR

Ursus arctos horribilis

🐾 **The grizzly bear is one subspecies of the** larger population of brown bears. The brown bear is probably second after the gray wolf in terms of how widespread its range once was: from Central Europe to the Great Plains of North America. Also like the wolf, the brown bear has been driven from much of that original range. The grizzly bear in particular could once be found from Alaska across the western part of the United States to Central Mexico. Now, it is largely gone from its range south of the Canadian border. This bear is an omnivore, with meat making up less than half of its diet. However, when certain prey is abundant, it will eat large quantities of that species of prey. This is an important part of the bear life cycle because they are hibernators and must store lots of fat for the winter.

🔭 **I find bears of any variety quite fascinating.** These large bears are often very inquisitive and appear to be very intelligent. They also seem very playful and can often be spotted splashing and playing in the pools in their enclosures. Like the American black bear, they come in a range of colors from blond to very dark brown, as you can see in the pictures on these pages. In the wild, grizzly bears eat a variety of different fruits and berries and, in captivity, seem to be quite fond of apples. These big bears must be well trained in zoos so keepers can safely perform checkups and see to their overall health. Keeper talks about bears tend to be some of the most popular in any zoo, as they demonstrate the techniques they use to help keep the bears healthy and happy.

CONSERVATION STATUS

CRITICALLY ENDANGERED   ENDANGERED   VULNERABLE   NEAR THREATENED   **LEAST CONCERN**

Grizzly bear from Chahinkapa Zoo in Wahpeton, ND

Grizzly bears from Great Plains Zoo in Sioux Falls, SD (above), and
Sedgwick County Zoo in Wichita, KS (below)

HIPPOPOTAMUS

Hippopotamus amphibius

The hippopotamus is the third largest land animal in Africa after the elephant and white rhinoceros. It is also the third most deadly animal in Africa, behind the mosquito and puff adder. These large herbivores spend most of their time in the water. However, they do not normally eat aquatic plants. Instead, they come ashore at night to feed on grass. They trim the grass close to the ground, enough so their feeding areas are often called "hippo lawns." Hippopotamuses are gregarious but not particularly social, living in groups of up to 30 individuals. The large bulls are very territorial and will defend the section of riverbank where he gathers a harem of females. The female hippopotamus is extremely protective and will threaten anything that gets between her and her baby. These characteristics, combined with their size and sharp teeth, are why they are among the most dangerous animals in Africa. They are under pressure because of agricultural activity, which is reducing the amount of water in the rivers where they live.

When seeing hippopotamuses lounging calmly in their pools, it can be hard to believe they are as dangerous as they are. I enjoy seeing them in the zoo because they require a big commitment on the zoo's part to care for them properly. They require large pools of water that must be cleaned every day, and they eat up to 150 pounds of food daily. Probably the most interesting thing is to watch them sleep in the water since they do not consciously breathe when they are underwater. They will rise to take a breath and submerge themselves again without ever waking up. I particularly like hippopotamuses because they have a variety of facial expressions, making them excellent animals to photograph.

CONSERVATION STATUS

CRITICALLY ENDANGERED	ENDANGERED	VULNERABLE	NEAR THREATENED	LEAST CONCERN

Hippopotamus from Sedgwick County Zoo in Wichita, KS

Hippopotamuses from Topeka Zoo in Topeka, KS (above), and Kansas City Zoo in Kansas City, MO (below)

HOFFMAN'S TWO-TOED SLOTH

Choloepus hoffmanni

There are two species of two-toed sloths, Hoffman's and Linnaeus's. In the wild, where their two ranges overlap, they are very difficult to tell apart. These sloths are not directly related to the three-toed sloths, the other family of sloths, which live in the same rain forests. In fact, the name "two-toed" is a bit of a misnomer. They only have two digits on their front limbs, while their back limbs have three. Life for the sloth happens in slow motion, with everything taking them a long time—even digestion, which sometimes takes up to a month. One interesting adaptation these sloths have is that their hair parts along their stomach so that rain drips off when they are hanging upside down.

Most of the sloths you see in zoos are the two-toed variety. Of the two families of sloths, they are the speedier and more alert. I really enjoy seeing these animals as they do not seem to have a care in the world other than finding a tasty morsel to snack on. Most of the time they are sleeping and will spend up to 18 hours a day napping to conserve energy. Although, the sloth pictured below from the Como Park Zoo seems to be more alert than most. Both times I have visited, he has been awake. On these pages, I have pictures of both species of two-toed sloths. I will leave it to the reader to see if they can tell them apart, but I will give a hint: the Linnaeus's sloth lives in Nebraska.

CONSERVATION STATUS

CRITICALLY ENDANGERED   ENDANGERED   VULNERABLE   NEAR THREATENED   **LEAST CONCERN**

Hoffman's two-toed sloth from Como Park Zoo in Saint Paul, MN

Linnaeus's two-toed sloth from Lincoln Children's Zoo in Lincoln, NE (above), and
Hoffman's two-toed sloth from Tanganyika Wildlife Park in Goddard, KS (below)

JAPANESE MACAQUE

Macaca fuscata

The Japanese macaque can only be found in Japan and is the northernmost monkey species. Like all macaques, these monkeys are well adapted to living in a variety of environments. For this species, that includes the cold and snow, which gives us their other name, snow monkeys. Japanese macaques are famous for one specific adaptation, which is the use of hot springs to warm themselves up during the winter. They are omnivores, primarily eating various plants, fruit, nuts, or bark. Their diet largely depends on where they live, which can range from subtropical forests in the south to subarctic forests in the north. These monkeys are highly intelligent primates and have been observed engaging in novel behaviors and passing those behaviors on to the benefit of their troops. These troops, like most other macaques, are matrilineal in nature, with males regularly leaving for other troops over their lifetimes.

In general, monkeys are fun to watch, and that is definitely the case for these monkeys, too. Japanese macaques seem quite fond of rough and tumble games of follow the leader or tag. The monkey seen in the picture below from Blank Park Zoo was engaged in a game of chicken with a couple of other younger monkeys from his troop. When not playing, Japanese macaques are foraging for food and treats left around the enclosure by their keepers or can be found just sitting and relaxing after a long morning of activity. These monkeys are rather common in zoos in the Midwest because they can tolerate a colder climate.

CONSERVATION STATUS

CRITICALLY ENDANGERED   ENDANGERED   VULNERABLE   NEAR THREATENED   **LEAST CONCERN**

Japanese macaque from Blank Park Zoo in Des Moines, IA

Japanese macaques from Great Plains Zoo in Sioux Falls, SD (above), and
Minnesota Zoo in Apple Valley, MN (below)

★ LION ★

Panthera leo

🐾 **The lion once ranged from the southern tip** of Africa to as far north as the southern border of Romania and from the west coasts of Africa to the east coasts of India. It is a very versatile big cat that can live in a variety of habitats from the desert's edge to all but the densest of rain forests. It is a powerful carnivore and is capable of taking down the largest of the African mega-fauna, including rhinoceroses and elephants. The lion is also the most social of the big cats and lives in close family groups called prides. These prides usually consist of a male and several females. Like most African wildlife, lions are under threat due to habitat loss and population fragmentation caused by increasing numbers of humans encroaching upon their territories. They are also under renewed threat from poaching and conflict with human farmers.

🔭 **Lions are one of the most laid-back animals at** the zoo. In the wild, they can spend up to 20 hours a day resting, which is why in the zoo they are most likely to be found lying down in a nice shady spot observing the world. In the spring and fall, it is not uncommon to see lions sunning themselves on a rock, much like a lizard. Since they are very social animals, they can sometimes be observed playing with each other, particularly younger lions. Lions are definitely on my list of animals I enjoy photographing, especially the big males with their large, impressive manes. Not to mention that when these big male lions roar in the zoo, it can often be heard for miles.

CONSERVATION STATUS

| CRITICALLY ENDANGERED | ENDANGERED | VULNERABLE | NEAR THREATENED | LEAST CONCERN |

Lion from Lake Superior Zoo in Duluth, MN

Lions from Henry Doorly Zoo in Omaha, NE (above), and Sedgwick County Zoo in Wichita, KS (below)

★ LLAMA ★

Lama glama

🐾 **The llama is the only domesticated species** included in this photo book. The modern llama is descended from the wild guanaco with some inter-mixing with the alpaca. It is believed that llamas were first domesticated nearly 7000 years ago high up in the mountains of northwest Argentina and northern Chile. Domestication occurred independently in other locations, like Peru, not long after. The llama is kept as a pack animal and for its wool, which is lanolin-free and used to make a wide variety of items depending on the coarseness of the fiber. Rougher wool is used to make rugs, and finer wool is used to make clothes and crafts. At one time only raised in South America, the llama is now an important farm animal in the United States and Canada as well.

🔭 **Llamas are nearly ubiquitous in zoos these** days, whether in the petting area or in their own exhibit. They have always reminded me of a character from a Spaghetti Western. All they need is the cowboy hat and poncho, which is easy to imagine on the llama in the picture below from Chahinkapa Zoo. They are usually very tame animals and interact well with children, which is important for an animal in the petting area. Often in the summer, they will be shaved, so they do not overheat on warm days. Whatever else might be said about llamas, they have exceptionally cute babies. And, when I am taking pictures, they are usually very interested in me and my camera.

CONSERVATION STATUS

CRITICALLY ENDANGERED   ENDANGERED   VULNERABLE   NEAR THREATENED   **DOMESTICATED**

Llama from Chahinkapa Zoo in Wahpeton, ND

Llamas from Roosevelt Park Zoo in Minot, ND (above), and Minnesota Zoo in Apple Valley, MN (below)

MALAYAN TAPIR

Tapirus indicus

🐾 **The Malayan tapir is the only species of tapir** native to Asia, with the other three being from South America. It is also the biggest of the four species of tapir, measuring about three and a half feet tall at the shoulders. They are native to the Malay Peninsula and the island Sumatra, as well as small pockets in Thailand. When born, the babies have stripes and spots rather than the familiar black-and-white pattern of adults. Malayan tapirs grow into their adult colors at about five months old. They spend much of their time in water and only come ashore for brief periods to eat and sleep. They are herbivores and eat mostly leaves, often knocking down smaller trees to get them. Because of their large size, Malayan tapirs are rarely a target for large predators, so humans are their only real threat. Their numbers are declining in the wild due to deforestation and, to a limited extent, hunting.

👀 **The Malayan tapir is instantly recognizable** because of its black-and-white coloring and long nose. In the wild, it uses this long nose to forage for food and smell its environment. In the picture below from Minnesota Zoo, the snout can be seen quite clearly. A baby tapir, who was about six months old at the time, can be seen as well. Provided all goes well, a baby will live about 30 years or so in both captivity and in the wild. I always enjoy seeing Malayan tapirs in the zoo, though they are quite rare, with only 37 individuals living in zoos in North America. This makes the Midwest rather special as three zoos in this region have them.

CONSERVATION STATUS

CRITICALLY ENDANGERED | **ENDANGERED** | VULNERABLE | NEAR THREATENED | LEAST CONCERN

Malayan tapirs from Minnesota Zoo in Apple Valley, MN

152

Malayan tapirs from Sedgwick County Zoo in Wichita, KS (above), and
Henry Doorly Zoo in Omaha, NE (below)

MANED WOLF

Chrysocyon brachyurus

With the looks of a large red fox on stilts, the maned wolf is neither a wolf or a fox. In fact, it is the only living member of the genus *Chrysocyon*. It appears it separated from the main branch of canids, the family of dogs and wolves, relatively early in its evolution, and its closest living relative is the bush dog. While technically a carnivore, this species actually feeds more on plants and fruits than on animals. It is particularly fond of the wolf apple, a member of the nightshade family, which also includes tomatoes and eggplants. These fruits may make up more than half of the maned wolf's diet in areas where it is plentiful. Unlike most canids, maned wolves are solitary animals that only interact during the breeding season, though a mated pair will often share a joint territory. These animals are under serious threat from human activity, particularly due to habitat loss caused by agriculture and diseases from domesticated dogs.

I read somewhere in researching these animals that once you see them, you will quickly fall in love with them. I know I was certainly very pleased to be introduced to maned wolves and see more of them on my journeys across the Midwest. Because relatively few zoos can provide them with a home all to themselves, they can be found more and more in mixed-species exhibits. This mimics where they come from in the wild, and so they will often be housed with giant anteaters or tapirs. The maned wolf pictured below from Sunset Zoo was in just such an enclosure, sharing it with a giant anteater that is also pictured in this book.

CONSERVATION STATUS

CRITICALLY ENDANGERED   ENDANGERED   VULNERABLE   **NEAR THREATENED**   LEAST CONCERN

Maned wolf from Sunset Zoo in Manhattan, KS

Maned wolves from Sedgwick County Zoo in Wichita, KS (above), and Lee Richardson Zoo in Garden City, KS (below)

MEERKAT

Suricata suricatta

The meerkat is a small member of the mongoose family. They can be found south of a line drawn from the southwest corner of Angola to the northernmost coast of South Africa. The meerkat shares this range with another small member of the mongoose family, the yellow mongoose. In fact, they can sometimes be found living together in the same burrows. Meerkats are insectivores and eat a wide variety of arthropods, with scorpions being a particular delicacy for them. They are a social species that live in groups called mobs that can number from 20 to 30 individuals, all of whom are usually related. The younger females will often take care of their baby siblings, protecting them and teaching them to hunt. Other mob members may have other jobs, such as sentry duty. Sentries watch for predators and alarm the group loudly if one approaches their territory.

Meerkats are on my top 10 list of favorite animals to see at the zoo. They are often scampering around their enclosures doing meerkat things, like standing guard or digging. When they are not doing these things, they are just as likely to be sitting in the sun relaxing. Like some of the other animals I have photographed, they are very interested in my camera and what I am doing. They will often get as close as they can to check me and my camera out to make sure we are not up to any funny business. Best of all, they are absolutely adorable little balls of fluff when they are babies.

CONSERVATION STATUS

CRITICALLY ENDANGERED   ENDANGERED   VULNERABLE   NEAR THREATENED   **LEAST CONCERN**

Meerkats from Hemker Park and Zoo in Freeport, MN

156

Meerkats from Henry Doorly Zoo in Omaha, NE (above), and Sedgwick County Zoo in Wichita, KS (below)

NORTH AMERICAN RIVER OTTER

Lontra canadensis

🐾 The North American river otter has a range that encompasses most of North America from Florida to Alaska. The river otter is a predator that preys predominantly on fish but also on amphibians, reptiles, birds, and small mammals. They are unique in that their right lung is larger than their left lung, which may aid in swimming underwater. Even though they are called river otters, they inhabit a wide variety of ecosystems, from rivers to marshlands and even coastal shorelines. River otters, like most other otters, are social creatures, living in either family groups of a female and her offspring or in bachelor groups composed of several unrelated males. The biggest threat to the North American river otter is from man-made pollution. In heavily polluted areas, otters have virtually disappeared.

🔭 I have loved otters for as long as I can remember. They always seem to be having so much fun. They are also very smart and very inquisitive. When I take pictures of them, they are always extremely interested in what I am doing, at least if they are awake. Otters spend a great deal of time sleeping as they are predators and need to conserve energy. When they are not sleeping, they like to play and have fun. For instance, the North American river otter at Dakota Zoo likes to do back flips when people are watching. You can see it mid-flip in the picture on the opposite page. This is a common behavior in the wild, too, where one of the favorite games they play is chase, and often the entire family group will be involved in the game.

CONSERVATION STATUS

CRITICALLY ENDANGERED   ENDANGERED   VULNERABLE   NEAR THREATENED   **LEAST CONCERN**

North American river otter from Blank Park Zoo in Des Moines, IA

North American river otters from Dickerson Park Zoo in Springfield, MO (above), and
Dakota Zoo in Bismarck, ND (below)

North American river otters from Red River Zoo in Fargo, ND (above), and Kansas City Zoo in Kansas City, MO (below)

North American river otters from Minnesota Zoo in Apple Valley, MN (above), and
Bramble Park Zoo in Watertown, SD (below)

★ OKAPI ★

Okapia johnstoni

🐾 The okapi is a shy forest-dwelling member of the giraffe family. It is native to the tropical forests of the Democratic Republic of the Congo, which is the only place they can be found. The okapi is an herbivore and is known to browse on over 100 different species of plants and fungi. It uses its 18-inch tongue to get the best leaves from trees and bushes. Originally, the okapi was thought to be something of a myth to the Europeans living in Africa during colonial times. It was not until 1901 that the species was described for science when a specimen was returned to Europe for study. In large part, this is due to their shy and solitary nature. Unlike giraffes, they do not live in groups and only socialize for mating. The okapi is now under threat from the civil war in the country as well as from illegal mining operations and illegal hunting for the bushmeat trade.

🔭 Because of their shy nature, it is sometimes very difficult to get a good picture of an okapi. But because I think they are such beautiful and strange animals, I am always just happy to spot them in their enclosure. They look like someone pieced them together by committee, with a part from this animal and another part from that animal. Their heads look like a giraffe's, but only males have giraffe-like horns, so it is easy to tell the sexes apart. Otherwise, okapis have striped legs, much like a zebra, and the body of a large deer. They are truly rare in American zoos, with only about 25 having them on exhibit. Fortunately for me, five of those zoos are in the Midwest, including, until just recently, my home zoo, Blank Park Zoo. I was sad to hear the okapi at my home zoo passed away in the summer of 2019 after being injured.

CONSERVATION STATUS

CRITICALLY ENDANGERED | **ENDANGERED** | VULNERABLE | NEAR THREATENED | LEAST CONCERN

Okapi from Saint Louis Zoo in Saint Louis, MO

Okapis from Henry Doorly Zoo in Omaha, NE (above), and Sedgwick County Zoo in Wichita, KS (below)

★ OSTRICH ★

Struthio camelus

The main claim to fame for the ostrich is that it is the largest living bird. It shares a lot in common with its close relative the emu, which is also in this book. Like the emu, the male is the primary incubator of the eggs. The ostrich mainly eats plants but will, on occasion, dine on insects and other invertebrates. There are three living subspecies of ostrich, among which the North African ostrich is considered critically endangered. This subspecies lives across the middle of Africa in a region known as the Sahel, the transition zone between the Sahara Desert to the north and the tropical forests and savannas to the south. The largest of the three subspecies, the North African ostrich can now only be found in isolated pockets in the central part of its former range. However, conservation efforts throughout North Africa are working diligently to reintroduce this endangered subspecies in many parts of its former range.

Ostriches have always seemed a bit odd to me. Like emus and rheas, they always strike me as some sort of giant chicken on stilts. They are often very interesting to watch as they prance around their enclosures looking for food. Occasionally, they give a brief glimpse of the speeds they can obtain, namely up to 40 miles per hour, but most of the time, they are content to go at a slow pace, eating and then resting for most of the day. While telling the different subspecies apart can be a challenge, telling the difference between male and female ostriches is easy. The females, like the one pictured opposite from Henry Doorly Zoo, are grayish-brown, while the males are much darker, nearly black, in coloring.

CONSERVATION STATUS

| CRITICALLY ENDANGERED | ENDANGERED | VULNERABLE | NEAR THREATENED | LEAST CONCERN |

Ostriches from Como Park Zoo in Saint Paul, MN

Ostriches from Henry Doorly Zoo in Omaha, NE (above), and Saint Louis Zoo in Saint Louis, MO (below)

PRONGHORN

Antilocapra americana

The pronghorn is the only living member of the superfamily Giraffoidea in North America. The other living members are the giraffe and okapi, both of which are native to Africa. The pronghorn is the second fastest land animal, achieving speeds over 55 miles per hour for short bursts. It is thought that they evolved to attain this speed to evade the American cheetah, also from North America and a now extinct cat that was only distantly related to modern cheetahs. Pronghorns are herbivores that eat mainly flowering plants and shrubs, depending on their local environment. Because of this, they rarely compete with other species, such as bison, deer, or domestic cattle for food. Historically, the pronghorn was endangered due to overhunting but has since recovered. The main pressures on the animal now are habitat fragmentation and blockage of traditional migration routes.

Pronghorns are rather homely creatures, but there is still something beautiful about them. When they move, they are very graceful and the speed they are capable of is quite apparent. Being one of the fastest land animals, they are always on my list of animals I want to see at the zoo. Unfortunately, zoos rarely have the room for pronghorns to really let loose, so I am looking forward to an eventual trip to a national park out West to see them go all out. I really enjoy taking pictures of pronghorns simply because they are so different from most of the other animals in the zoo. One extraordinary thing about them is their eyes. Like most prey species, their eyes are set on the side of the head to give them excellent all-around vision, while most predators have forward-facing eyes for good depth perception. In the case of this animal, they have a 320-degree field of vision, so just a few degrees shy of a complete circle around themselves.

CONSERVATION STATUS

| CRITICALLY ENDANGERED | ENDANGERED | VULNERABLE | NEAR THREATENED | LEAST CONCERN |

Pronghorn from Lee Richardson Zoo in Garden City, KS

Pronghorns from Hemker Park and Zoo in Freeport, MN (above), and Topeka Zoo in Topeka, KS (below)

PRZEWALSKI'S HORSE

Equus ferus przewalskii

Przewalski's horse is something of a miracle of conservation. They were extinct in the wild in the 1960s, but through good management of zoo populations, they were reintroduced into the wild in 1992. This wild horse was once native to Mongolia and the bordering areas of Russia and China. It is believed to be one of the most primitive species of wild horse but is not directly related to domestic horses. Przewalski's horses are herbivores that eat a variety of plants, and in the wild, they seem to enjoy seasonal favorites. This horse is well adapted to the cold steppes where it lives and migrates to different regions within its range to follow the availability of the nutritious plants it eats. While it has been successfully reintroduced into the wild, Przewalski's horse is still under pressure from human activities, such as agriculture and mining.

I am always excited to see these wild horses in a zoo because it gives me hope that other critically endangered or extinct-in-the-wild animals, like the scimitar-horned oryx, might be successfully reintroduced back into the wild one day. I particularly like the stiff mane these horses have; it reminds me of the mohawk I had in my younger days. Przewalski's horses are like other horses in that they seem quite happy to wander around their enclosures, munching on grass and getting a good dust bath when it all gets to be too much. Because conservation efforts in zoos have been very successful, you will often get a chance to see a cute baby foal when you visit. This wild horse is on my list of animals I really want to go visit in the wild. And hopefully, with the conservation efforts on its behalf, they will continue to be there for me to see.

CONSERVATION STATUS

| CRITICALLY ENDANGERED | ENDANGERED | VULNERABLE | NEAR THREATENED | LEAST CONCERN |

Przewalski's horse from Lee Richardson Zoo in Garden City, KS

Przewalski's horses from Dakota Zoo in Bismarck, ND (above), and Minnesota Zoo in Apple Valley, MN (below)

RED KANGAROO

Macropus rufus

The red kangaroo is found throughout most of Australia. It is the largest living marsupial and the largest of all kangaroos as well. Though called the red kangaroo, they can come in a range of colors, particularly females who are more likely to be grayish in color. The red kangaroo is an herbivore that eats mostly grasses that grow around watering holes. With no natural predators still in existence, these animals spend most of their day either grazing or resting out of the hot sun. However, they still have the speed they once used to avoid predators and can hop at speeds upward of 40 miles per hour over short distances. Like all marsupials, the babies of red kangaroos are born very underdeveloped and crawl into their mother's pouch to finish growing.

The kangaroo has always reminded me of an overgrown rabbit and the red kangaroo particularly so. Most of the time in zoos, they are found lying down resting, just like they would be in the wild. It is fun just seeing them chilling in the shade, but viewing them when they are active, usually in the mornings or evenings, is even better. Watching them hop around their enclosures really shows all the adaptations kangaroos have, like their elastic Achilles tendon. This tendon actually stretches like a rubber band and propels them into their next hop. One of the best places to see red kangaroos is in the Australian area of the Kansas City Zoo where they are free to roam in a large field you can walk through, too.

CONSERVATION STATUS

CRITICALLY ENDANGERED   ENDANGERED   VULNERABLE   NEAR THREATENED   **LEAST CONCERN**

Red kangaroos from Kansas City Zoo in Kansas City, MO

Red kangaroos from Bramble Park Zoo in Watertown, SD (above), and Roosevelt Park Zoo in Minot, ND (below)

★ RED PANDA ★

Ailurus fulgens

The red panda is native to a range from Southwest China to Nepal. It is not actually a bear but part of the large superfamily Musteloidea, which includes weasels and raccoons. The red panda is primarily threatened by habitat loss and fragmentation and also by poaching. It lives in cool temperate forests at an altitude of 7200 to 15,700 feet where there is little variation in temperature from its preferred range of 50 to 77 degrees. The red panda primarily eats bamboo, hence the early incorrect association with the giant panda, but supplements this with a variety of other plants and mushrooms. Occasionally red pandas are also carnivores or insectivores. One thing these animals have in common with the giant panda is a false thumb used for arboreal movement. They developed this independently, and it is a good example of convergent evolution.

Red pandas are one of my favorite animals to see at the zoo. Since they seem to be very adaptable to living in captivity, they go about their business unbothered by people watching them, which for the most part means eating and sleeping. They enjoy napping high up off the ground, so looking up is usually required to see them. The most fun I had with a red panda was at the Red River Zoo when it took me nearly 20 minutes to get just a few good pictures. It seemed like he was almost deliberately trying to avoid the camera. It turns out this particular one, named Sheffield, is something of an escape artist, having escaped his enclosure several times.

CONSERVATION STATUS

CRITICALLY ENDANGERED   **ENDANGERED**   VULNERABLE   NEAR THREATENED   LEAST CONCERN

Red panda named Sheffield from Red River Zoo in Fargo, ND

Red pandas from Minnesota Zoo in Apple Valley, MN (above), and Kansas City Zoo in Kansas City, MO (below)

Red pandas from Hemker Park and Zoo in Freeport, MN (above), and Saint Louis Zoo in Saint Louis, MO (below)

Red pandas from Great Plains Zoo in Sioux Falls, SD (above), and Henry Doorly Zoo in Omaha, NE (below)

★ RED RIVER HOG ★

Potamochoerus porcus

The red river hog is a member of the pig family who lives in the rain forests of western Central Africa. It prefers living near water, such as rivers and swamps. They typically live in small family groups of a male, several females, and their young. However, they sometimes aggregate into large herds of 60 individuals or more. They are omnivores that feed primarily on roots and tubers but may eat carrion, insects, and lizards when the opportunity presents itself. Their range overlaps in some places with those of three of their cousins, namely the warthog, giant forest hog, and bushpig. While the conservation status of the species overall is categorized as least concern, there are many areas where the red river hog is under threat, especially from overhunting and habitat loss.

The red river hog was one of the new species I discovered during my travels around the zoos of the Midwest. Having never seen one before, I have enjoyed getting to know more about them. They are a moderately active animal in the mornings and evenings but prefer to rest and sleep during other parts of the day. If I make an early or late trip to the zoo, I can usually catch them doing something interesting. When they are active they enjoy rooting around in there enclosures looking for a tasty snack or playfully bothering their companions. I especially like their reddish-orange color and large snouts, which make them very photogenic. The picture below, from the Kansas City Zoo, is from my first time encountering these delightful creatures.

CONSERVATION STATUS

CRITICALLY ENDANGERED   ENDANGERED   VULNERABLE   NEAR THREATENED   **LEAST CONCERN**

Red river hog from Kansas City Zoo in Kansas City, MO

Red river hogs from Sedgwick County Zoo in Wichita, KS (above), and
Saint Louis Zoo in Saint Louis, MO (below)

★ RING-TAILED LEMUR ★

Lemur catta

🐾 The ring-tailed lemur is a larger member of the lemur family. Like all lemurs, they are only found on the island of Madagascar. These lemurs are easily recognizable by their bushy striped tail and cat-like face. They are unique among the lemurs in that they spend a good deal of time on the ground, especially when moving from place to place. However, they are still arboreal creatures and spend most of their time up in the canopy of their forest home. The ring-tailed lemur is an omnivore, but most of its diet is plant-based. Its favorite food is the fruit of the tamarind tree. This species and the rest of the lemur family are under extreme pressure from habitat destruction and poaching.

🔭 Ring-tailed lemurs have always been one of my favorite animals to see at the zoo. The best time to see them is in the first part of the day when you can usually find them doing their morning "sun worship." They will sit on the ground facing the sun and stretch out to soak up its warmth. That is how I found the lemur from Bramble Park Zoo in the picture below. Ring-tailed lemurs also like being in cuddle piles for strengthening social bonds and for mutual warmth. Even though they are endangered in the wild, there are more ring-tailed lemurs in zoos than in Madagascar. If the worst case scenario possible comes to be, there will be a way to reintroduce them thanks to zoos.

CONSERVATION STATUS

CRITICALLY ENDANGERED · **ENDANGERED** · VULNERABLE · NEAR THREATENED · LEAST CONCERN

Ring-tailed lemur from Bramble Park Zoo in Watertown, SD

Ring-tailed lemurs from Great Plains Zoo in Sioux Falls, SD (above), and David Traylor Zoo in Emporia, KS (below)

SICHUAN TAKIN

Budorcas taxicolor tibetana

The Sichuan, or Tibetan, takin is one of four subspecies of takin. They are native to the Eastern Himalayas in China and Tibet. They share their home range with giant pandas, red pandas, and several of their cousins from the suborder Caprinae, called goat antelopes. These large herbivores are not very picky eaters and will dine on everything from grass to bamboo shoots to oak leaves. Sichuan takins are highly adapted to the cold climate they live in and seasonally migrate up and down the mountains to find better feeding grounds. All takins are under a great deal of pressure, mainly from illegal hunting, but habitat loss is also a contributing factor. Their long term survival is being aided by conservation efforts for the giant panda and golden monkey.

The Sichuan takin is another animal I learned about in my travels for this book, and they rapidly became one of my favorites to see in the zoo. I am particularly lucky in that regard because most of the zoos where they live are either in the Midwest or Great Lakes region. In fact, of the 18 zoos in the United States that have these wonderful animals, a total of 12 are located in these regions. I think Sichuan takins are amazing to watch because they look like someone randomly put different animal parts together to make them. They have a giant nose, which is used to warm cold air when they breathe, and their face rather resembles that of a moose. Their shaggy coat is covered in an oily substance that repels rain and snow.

CONSERVATION STATUS

| CRITICALLY ENDANGERED | ENDANGERED | VULNERABLE | NEAR THREATENED | LEAST CONCERN |

Sichuan takin from Red River Zoo in Fargo, ND

Sichuan takins from Minnesota Zoo in Apple Valley, MN (above), and
Lee Richardson Zoo in Garden City, KS (below)

★ SNOW LEOPARD ★

Panthera uncia

🐾 **The snow leopard is the smallest member of** the big cat family, *Panthera*. Based on DNA analysis, it is believed to be most like the original ancestors of the big cats. It can be found in the Himalayas in India, across the Tibetan Plateau, and in the mountainous parts of Eastern Mongolia and south-central Russia. This big cat is a mountain expert and normally spends most of its time at altitudes greater than 9000 feet above sea level. It is very well adapted to its cold environment with broad paws for walking on snow and a long, thick bushy tail, which can cover its face when it sleeps. The biggest threat to the snow leopard is illegal hunting for their fur and of the prey species they rely on. They are also under threat because of a shrinking habitat due to global warming.

🔭 **These beautiful fluffy cats are a regular in** zoos, and they are my favorite big cat to see. Like most big carnivores, they spend most of their day snoozing and are usually only active in the morning and evening. Oftentimes, spotting these animals requires looking up, as they seem to like being high up off the ground on the rocks in their enclosure. One of the best places to see a snow leopard is at the Great Plains Zoo. The enclosure there provides lots of ledges and nooks for a snow leopard to hide and sleep while still giving spectators a pretty good view. The snow leopard is another animal that I am looking forward to seeing in their natural habitat someday, but that may be a tall order because they are shy and elusive in the wild.

CONSERVATION STATUS

CRITICALLY ENDANGERED   ENDANGERED   VULNERABLE   NEAR THREATENED   LEAST CONCERN

Snow leopard from Henry Doorly Zoo in Omaha, NE

Snow leopards from Great Plains Zoo in Sioux Falls, SD (above), and
Lincoln Children's Zoo in Lincoln, NE (below)

TAMMAR WALLABY

Macropus eugenii

The tammar wallaby is one of the smaller species of wallaby, only reaching an average height of about 18 inches. They can be found in isolated pockets in the southwestern part of Australia and on Kangaroo Island near Adelaide. These wallabies are herbivores who mainly graze on grasses and flowers, though they will browse for leaves off lower branches of shrubs. They are marsupials, and like kangaroos, they give birth to a small underdeveloped baby, which then crawls into the mother's pouch to continue growing. It takes almost a year for the joey to fully develop and become independent. The biggest danger to this species of wallaby is predation by introduced red foxes and dingoes. The fox is of particular concern as they may eliminate the species from an area entirely by overhunting.

I find most wallabies to be very charming, and I enjoy seeing them in zoos. Outside of zoos, they have been a moderately successful species when they have been introduced in other locations, like England and Scotland. They seem to be able to adapt well to captivity and usually breed very well. The tammar wallaby, like other wallaby species, makes a very good model for photography, especially in walk-in enclosures where you can get very close to them. The very chubby wallaby in the picture below from Sedgwick County Zoo lives in just such an enclosure. It has rapidly become the norm for zoos to have a walk-through exhibit with kangaroos, wallabies, or both. The one at my home zoo, Blank Park Zoo, has wallabies and is very well done.

CONSERVATION STATUS

CRITICALLY ENDANGERED   ENDANGERED   VULNERABLE   NEAR THREATENED   **LEAST CONCERN**

Tammar wallaby from Sedgwick County Zoo in Wichita, KS

Tammar wallabies from Dakota Zoo in Bismarck, ND (above), and
Lincoln Children's Zoo in Lincoln, NE (below)

★ TRUMPETER SWAN ★

Cygnus buccinator

🐾 The trumpeter swan is the largest living waterbird and second largest bird capable of flight just after the Andean condor. Trumpeter swans are native to the United States and Canada, though in the late 1800s, they were nearly hunted to extinction in the lower 48 states, with only 70 birds left near Yellowstone National Park. They were saved from extinction in the 1950s when a previously unknown population of them was discovered on the Copper River in Alaska. These birds were then reintroduced in the lower 48 states. Even though the swan is out of danger for the moment, it faces new threats from global climate change, which is causing spring flooding of nesting sites. Like other swans, the trumpeter swan often mates for life, so they are commonly found in pairs. The egg of this swan is one of the largest eggs of any flying bird, weighing in at just over 11 ounces.

🔭 The trumpeter swan is a relatively common sight in zoos today. They can be found in nearly all the zoos I visited in the Midwest. Like the black swan mentioned earlier, there is something peaceful and serene about watching them glide through the water of their ponds. One of the best times to see these animals is in June or July because they will very likely have baby swans then, like the little cygnet pictured below from the Riverside Discovery Center. When the cygnets hatch, they are a light-gray color, and it will take nearly a year for them to develop their all-white adult plumage.

CONSERVATION STATUS

CRITICALLY ENDANGERED   ENDANGERED   VULNERABLE   NEAR THREATENED   **LEAST CONCERN**

Trumpeter swan from Riverside Discovery Center in Scottsbluff, NE

Trumpeter swans from David Traylor Zoo in Emporia, KS (above), and Great Bend-Brit Spaugh Zoo in Great Bend, KS (below)

WESTERN LOWLAND GORILLA

Gorilla gorilla gorilla

The western lowland gorilla is the most numerous of the four subspecies of gorilla and is the only subspecies found in zoos. These gorillas are native to western Central Africa, including Gabon, Cameroon, and the Republic of the Congo. Gorillas normally live in one of two kinds of groups, a family group led by a dominant silverback male with two to four females and juveniles or in an all-male bachelor group. These large apes are almost exclusively herbivores, with fruit being their favorite food. However, they will, from time to time, eat insects to supplement their diet with extra protein. Much like the chimpanzee, the gorilla is under threat of extinction because of human activity. They are being overhunted by poachers, driven from their homes by expanding human habitation, and are susceptible to many serious human illnesses, such as Ebola.

These large apes are fun to watch and observe, especially the young ones. They often play rough and tumble games with each other and often try to involve the leader of the group in their play, too. Gorillas require a great deal of space for their enclosures and are highly intelligent, so they also require plenty of enrichment activities. Oftentimes parts of their space will be covered with clover hay, which has been found to increase their well-being. Another interesting food they eat are the seeds from the grains of the paradise plant, which are believed to improve their cardiovascular health. Unlike chimpanzees, which can be loud and boisterous at times, gorillas are generally calm and not aggressive toward each other in mixed groups. Bachelor male groups may show more aggression towards each other.

CONSERVATION STATUS

CRITICALLY ENDANGERED   ENDANGERED   VULNERABLE   NEAR THREATENED   LEAST CONCERN

Western lowland gorilla from Sedgwick County Zoo in Wichita, KS

Western lowland gorillas from Henry Doorly Zoo in Omaha, NE (above), and Como Park Zoo in Saint Paul, MN (below)

★ PETTING ZOO ★

Also: Contact Area, Farm

Nearly every zoo included in this book has some type of animal contact area. They are usually home to a wide variety of domesticated animals, such as goats, sheep, llamas, and cows. While most of the zoo is hands-off, these areas are where hands-on is encouraged. This is important so that people can connect in a tactile way with animals at the zoo and hopefully gain some additional empathy not just for these domestic animals but for all animals in general. It is also the area where feeding animals is acceptable, as long as it is the food that the zoo has provided for them to be fed. Beyond these reasons, contact areas help connect people with the animals that we use to provide food on our dinner tables and fiber for the clothing we wear.

I always make it a point to stop at the animal contact areas in a zoo. I enjoy getting to see the animals and even pet a few. It is fun to see the joy on children's faces as they come face to face with an animal that is not only close but also one that they can touch and feed. Whether it is the Kids' Kingdom at my home zoo, Blank Park Zoo, the Family Farm at Minnesota Zoo, or the Children's Zoo Farm at Red River Zoo, they all provide a special place to interact with the animals and learn more about them. One of the most interesting ones is at Red River Zoo where they do not just have animals but also have a row crop exhibit where you can see what different crops, such as corn, wheat, and sunflowers, look like in person. The picture below shows one part of that exhibit, which is quite large and very well done.

CONSERVATION STATUS

CRITICALLY ENDANGERED   ENDANGERED   VULNERABLE   NEAR THREATENED   **DOMESTICATED**

Row crops at Red River Zoo in Fargo, ND

Goat from Sedgwick County Zoo in Wichita, KS (above), and
pig from Saint Louis Zoo in Saint Louis, MO (below)

Rabbit from Lincoln Children's Zoo in Lincoln, NE (above), and zebu from Blank Park Zoo in Des Moines, IA (below)

Miniature donkey from Chahinkapa Zoo in Wahpeton, ND (above), and sheep from Wright Park Zoo in Dodge City, KS (below)

Miniature horse from Great Plains Zoo in Sioux Falls, SD (above), and alpacas from Hemker Park and Zoo in Freeport, MN (below)

Chicken from Minnesota Zoo in Apple Valley, MN (above), and
Highland cow from Roosevelt Park Zoo in Minot, ND (below)

★ PHOTO INDEX ★

ZOOS

★ REFERENCES ★

INFORMATION ABOUT THE ZOOS WAS OBTAINED FROM THEIR
RESPECTIVE WEBSITES, THE WIKIPEDIA ARTICLES FOR EACH ZOO, AND
THE INTERNET ARCHIVE PAGES THAT HAVE BEEN SAVED FROM EACH
ZOO'S WEBSITE. ADDITIONAL INFORMATION WAS GATHERED THROUGH
EMAIL EXCHANGES AND PHONE CALLS WITH EACH OF THE ZOOS.

Zoos: see each zoo's page for their website information

Wikipedia: www.wikipedia.org

Internet Archive: www.archive.org

INFORMATION ABOUT THE ANIMALS PRESENTED IN THIS BOOK WAS
OBTAINED FROM THEIR WIKIPEDIA ARTICLES AND THE INTERNATIONAL
UNION FOR CONSERVATION OF NATURE AND NATURAL RESOURCES
(IUCN) RED LIST OF THREATENED SPECIES WEBSITE.

Wikipedia: www.wikipedia.org

IUCN Red List: www.iucnredlist.org

PLEASE CONSIDER GIVING GENEROUSLY TO ALL THESE INVALUABLE
INTERNET RESOURCES AND TO YOUR LOCAL ZOO.

Wikipedia: https://donate.wikimedia.org

IUCN Red List: www.iucnredlist.org/support/donate

Internet Archive: www.archive.org/donate

★ ABOUT THE AUTHOR ★

Stephen Toothman is a writer and photographer from the Midwest. When he is not traveling around the country taking pictures of zoos, he works as a programmer and system administrator. Aside from a fascination with photography and zoos, his other hobbies include computers and cooking. Wherever he travels, he always brings along "The Boys": Otter the otter, Redd the red panda, Charlie the ring-tailed lemur, and (not pictured) Pops the naughty monkey, who is actually a gorilla. They have been with him on all his trips over the last two years, and the gang is sure to grow over the coming years with even more zoo trips.

YOU CAN FOLLOW MY ADVENTURES AND SEE MORE ZOO PICTURES ON MY FACEBOOK PAGE, @ZOOSAPHOTOBOOKANDGUIDE, OR ON MY WEBSITE, WWW.ZOOS-APHOTOBOOKANDGUIDE.COM

Made in the USA
Monee, IL
06 November 2020